WHERE I AM

Heaven, Eternity, and Our Life Beyond the Now

Billy Graham

W PUBLISHING GROUP

AN IMPRINT OF THOMAS NELSON

Published in Nashville, Tennessee, by W Publishing Group, an imprint of Thomas Nelson.

Thomas Nelson titles may be purchased in bulk for educational, business, fund-raising, or sales promotional use. For information, please e-mail SpecialMarkets@ThomasNelson.com.

ISBN 978-0-7180-7750-1 (ITPE)

Library of Congress Control Number: 2015943085

ISBN 978-0-7180-4222-6

Printed in the United States of America

15 16 17 18 19 RRD 6 5 4 3 2 1

CONTENTS

THE NEW TESTAMENT

FOREWORD

Franklin Graham

WHILE HIS EARTHLY VISION DIMS, THE GLORY OF HEAVEN IS
ILLUMINATED AS MY FATHER, DR. BILLY GRAHAM, SHARES FROM
HIS PAST AND PRESENT THE REALITY OF ETERNITY IN HIS NEW
BOOK, *Where I Am*. While he no longer preaches from the stadiums of
the world, his heart still beats strong with the resounding assurance that
he will spend eternity with Jesus Christ, the Savior of the world, and he
still invites others to secure their eternal hope.

My father has always stayed in tune with world news—he still does—
and has said, "My heart breaks to see the world in such turmoil." We are
watching governments crumble; newscasters and people from around
the world are asking, "Is there anyone who can set the world on the right
track? Is there any hope? Where will it all end?"

Yes, there is hope, and when the end of this life comes, eternity will
be realized.

The CBS News program *Sunday Morning* reported the week before
Halloween 2014 that two-thirds of Americans believe in life after death,
either in Heaven or Hell, and most believe they can describe them both.
Yet their beliefs seldom, if ever, come from the Bible. So where do people
get their information on a real Heaven and a real Hell? CBS found that

most develop their visions of both places from the arts: from painters, musicians, films, and poets.[1]

Opinions on eternity, therefore, gain a hearing based on cultural conjecture rather than the time-tested truth of Scripture. This supports a popular theory that because God loves the whole world, He will change His nature to embrace the universal hope that all mankind will go to Heaven when they die. This is troublesome, however, for others who cannot possibly imagine a loving God allowing some of history's most vile criminals to gain the glory of Heaven.

The truth is: God does not change (Malachi 3:6), and He has prepared Heaven for those who believe and obey Him. He also has prepared a place for Satan, his demons, and all those who reject Christ.

Just after he completed his last book, *The Reason for My Hope: Salvation*,[2] my father immediately began drafting another book on the subject of eternity. "Death is the doorstep to eternity," he says. But this age-old subject is still debated after thousands of years. While the culture reflects an ongoing interest in the afterlife, few take it seriously enough to make the necessary plans to secure where they will spend "forever." The eternal affairs of mankind can only be determined by a decision made internally.

A longtime friend of ours, the late Zig Ziglar, wrote, "The good news is there is nothing we can do that is bad enough to keep us out of Heaven; the bad news is there is nothing we can do good enough to get us into Heaven."

My father has preached on this truth for seventy years, and it is the heart of this book. From his earliest outline for this book, my father envisioned that it would be fleshed out using his archival sermons that span his seven decades of preaching and written works. He now invites you to reflect on the questions and answers that ultimately lead the souls of mankind into death's tomorrow. From the beginning of God's Word to the end, he shines the light on the answers to people's questions: When does eternity begin? Where are the destinations? How do we get there? How long will it last?

As our nation and world travail in the midst of political, economic, and cultural uncertainties, readers will find comfort in the hope that comes from the unchanging truth of God's Word. This book is a gathering of God's promises by a man who is still a preacher of the Gospel of Jesus Christ.

You will catch glimpses into some of the conversations about eternity that my father has had with people from all walks of life. Whether talking with a world leader, the media, or the common man, my father always begins his answers to their questions with "The Bible says . . ." Now he shares what the Scripture says about eternity from all sixty-six books of the Bible. Each short chapter examines the biblical reality that mankind chooses where to spend life after death.

From the Old Testament writer who wrote, "[God] has also set eternity in their heart" (Ecclesiastes 3:11 NASB) to the New Testament writer who penned these words about Jesus: "Whoever believes in Him should not perish but have everlasting life" (John 3:16), there is hope for everyone who will put their faith and trust in the One who gives us this promise: "*Where I am*, there you may be also."

When asked, "Where is Heaven?" my father once wisely replied, "Heaven is where Jesus Christ is, and I'm going to Him soon." This thought prompted the title *Where I Am*, taken from Jesus' words of comfort: "Let not your heart be troubled; you believe in God, believe also in Me. . . . I go to prepare a place for you. . . . I will come again and receive you to Myself; that *where I am*, there you may be also" (14:1–4).

My father has said with resolve, "When I die, tell others that I've gone to my Lord and Savior Jesus Christ—that's *where I am*."

INTRODUCTION

MOST PEOPLE ACCEPT THAT HEAVEN IS REAL, ACCORDING TO A FOX NEWS POLL.[1] Many—religious and nonreligious—believe they will go there because God is a God of love.

Many of these same people, however, reject that Hell is real. Yet they reserve Hell as a very real place for people who have perpetrated some of the most hideous crimes in history and have absolutely no remorse in wanting some of the most infamous criminals to "go to Hell."

What does it reveal about people's hearts when they want someone condemned to Hell? They are obviously judging that person's actions against their own merit. They believe they are good enough to pass judgment on another person, but they accuse God—who is holy—of condemning people to this foreboding place.

"Please . . . write on anything but Hell!" This comes from bloggers in cyberspace who claim to be Christians. Responding to those who are sounding the warning about Hell, they write, "This makes Christians look like they serve a God filled with anger and wrath."

The Bible clearly states of those who do not believe what it says, Satan has blinded their eyes and muted their hearing (2 Corinthians 4:3–5). Meanwhile, these nonbelievers brag and make light of the fact that they look forward to going to Hell, where they will enjoy their works of evil without the righteousness of God hovering over them.

The reality is that none of us will ever escape the righteousness of God. The psalmist wrote:

> Where can I go from Your Spirit?
> Or where can I flee from Your presence?
> If I ascend into heaven, You are there;
> If I make my bed in hell, behold, You are there.
> (Psalm 139:7–8)

While we cannot escape the righteous judgment of God, it is also true that God, in His mercy and grace, wants to impart His righteousness through salvation to all people. Yet there are those who refuse such a gift.

So why do people want to close their eyes to the idea of Hell when the world is talking, blogging, and writing about a literal place that intrigues and inflames such passion? Hell is not an idea, a figment of the imagination, or the setting for a horror movie. It is the hideous reality that awaits those who refuse to let God come into their lives and make them new creations, filled with His forgiveness and love.

Please hear this truth: you will not escape God's righteousness by going to Hell.

Consider this: Multitudes do not flinch when they condemn to Hell people such as Saudi Arabia's Osama bin Laden, Germany's Adolf Hitler, or Cambodia's Pol Pot; or notorious Americans, such as Jeffrey Dahmer or Ted Bundy. Their accusers do not hesitate to suggest that certain people who have "stepped over the line" of what they consider evil will land in Hell when life on earth is over. In the next breath, however, many will say, "I do not believe that God would send good people to Hell."

Herein lies the problem—we see ourselves as good and refuse to see that we, too, harbor wickedness within. As the Bible says,

> The heart is deceitful above all things,
> And desperately wicked;
> Who can know it? (Jeremiah 17:9)

And further: "From within, out of the heart of men, proceed evil thoughts, adulteries, fornications, murders, thefts, covetousness, wickedness, deceit, lewdness, an evil eye, blasphemy, pride, foolishness. All these evil things come from within and defile a man" (Mark 7:21–23). You see, God does not play favorites. The sin of pride is in the same sentence as the sin of murder.

Where do you fit in? Are you like the rich young ruler who declared to Jesus that he had lived a perfect life? Or perhaps you feel only certain sins merit Hell. It does not really matter how we think of it; the truth of the Bible is what matters. And God's Word proclaims that all people are sinners. God—not man—has set the standard, and we all fall short.

The bloggers I mentioned earlier stated emphatically that no murderer should go to Heaven. The Bible says, "The Son of Man must be delivered into the hands of sinful [people], and be crucified, and the third day rise again" (Luke 24:7). Who are these sinful people? You and me. Our sins nailed Jesus Christ to the cross, and we have His blood on our hands. But God wants the blood of His Son to cover the sin in our hearts. This is why He came. Jesus looked down on mankind and said, "I love you with an everlasting love; repent of your sin and follow Me that *where I am* going you may also go."

Many people teach today that the blood of Jesus covers all sin, regardless of whether the sinner repents or not. This is Satan's great lie. Some believe they will automatically walk into Heaven when this earthly life is over because God is love. That would negate the sacrifice Jesus made on the cross. Don't be deceived, for God is not mocked. God is also a God of justice and righteousness. He is not preparing a place in Heaven for unrepentant sinners. While we have contributed nothing to God's free gift of salvation, there is a condition to possessing it—we must confess our sin, turn from it, and receive Christ on His terms.

This truth is repulsive to many. The pride that flaunts our self-proclaimed innocence is the very evidence of our guilt. Continuing in rebellion against God, whether the sin be pride or murder, will send souls to Hell. Then there will be no turning back, no second chances. There is no afterthought in the afterlife. Today is the time to decide where you will live forever—either Heaven or Hell. This may very well be an unpopular teaching, but popularity polls do not determine destiny for anyone.

What will be your eternal destination after this earthly life is over for you? Are you going to Heaven—or to Hell? This is the most important question you will ever face. I pray you will answer it honestly and that you will know the reason behind it. If you say that you will go to Heaven because you are good, the Bible says, "There is none who does good, no, not one" (Romans 3:12).

So if no one is good and Heaven is filled with only the righteous, who will be there? The answer is found in salvation—for God desires that all people be saved. Those who repent of sin against God, receive His forgiveness, and live in obedience to Him, God sees through the righteousness of His Son, the Lord Jesus Christ, who is preparing a place in Heaven for those who belong to Him. This is the goodness of Heaven. But those who reject His love, those who are not willing to turn their backs on evil and look to Him as their Master, God in His righteousness must judge them if they decide to remain in their sins and self-pleasure, choosing Hell for themselves.

The doom of Hell was not intended for human beings. God created us for fellowship with Him, though many have turned their backs on Him. Hell was created for the devil and his demons, and Satan wants to take the world with him into this diabolical place.

Don't think for one minute that Hell will be the "hottest" happy hour of all. Those who find themselves there will remember the hour of decision that determined their fate; they will face the inferno of God's wrath that will last not for an hour but for all the never-ending hours of forever.

This may sound like a scare tactic, but the discussion rages with many. "I'm not sure whether I believe in Hell," a young person wrote. "Guess I'll find out when life comes to an end." Here is a warning: the soul will never come to an end because eternity reaches out to each of us, extending our lives beyond the grave.

How do I know? The Bible says so, and God's truth is revealed in

His Word. Still people ask: Is there an afterlife, and if so where does it lead us?

There are many people offering answers, and this is a great problem. Many answers are deceiving and will lead people right into Hell, the very place they are told does not exist. Some say that people in Hell will make restitution and then be allowed into Heaven. Others counsel that perhaps the Hellbound will eventually be annihilated, put out of the misery of having to face the fact that they took the wrong road.

"Hell," some say, "is what Christians have used to scare people into converting to Christ." But is this really true? Did Jesus use scare tactics? No. Every word that proceeds out of the mouth of God is truth. Jesus spoke the truth because of His deep love for us. If the truth scares you, know that it is your guilty conscience reacting to Truth.

The world wonders about Hell every day. It is one of the most daunting and repeated topics seen in art, read in literature, debated among educators, and heard in music. David Clayton-Thomas of the 1970s rock band Blood, Sweat & Tears famously sang Heaven didn't exist, but still he prayed there wasn't a Hell.[2] But that was a futile prayer.

One blog took on the subject of Heaven and Hell. As people weighed in, the discussion became a vicious cycle. Finally one commenter frantically typed in, "Could someone please explain how to avoid Hell?"

Another asked, "How do you spell Hell?"

The flippant reply was, "Hoping Evil Lives Long."

But the Bible spells it this way: Hopelessly Everlasting, Literally Loveless.

You may be thinking, *Billy, surely you do not believe all of this Hellfire and brimstone!* My dear friends, it is not what I say that counts; it is what the Word of God says. Jesus spoke more about Hell than Heaven. Why? Because of His great compassion for souls. He gave His life to spare you the agony, torment, and gruesome reality that Hell is reserved for those who reject Christ.

Why would you choose this road to Hell? Be careful not to blame holy God for your own selfish choice to live any way you please on earth and then expect Him to welcome you into His beautiful heavenly home. He has provided the way of escape. We can be rescued from Hell only on this side of life, not in the afterlife.

Hell has been cloaked in folklore and disguised in fiction for so long that many people deny the reality of such a place. Books and articles have been written denying the doctrine of Hell—some have been bestsellers because they teach views of Hell and biblical descriptions as symbolism. Such misleading teachings make people feel more comfortable and take the worry out of what happens after death. But these people will never be able to hold the writers accountable for pointing them down the wrong road when they arrive in the very real destination the Bible describes.

Join me in these brief chapters as we explore together what the Bible says about the two roads to eternity. I can tell you this: not one word about Hell in the Bible would ever make you want to go there. And no one who understands the peace of Heaven would ever want to end up anywhere else. As Scripture puts it, "He who believes on Him will by no means be put to shame" (1 Peter 2:6).

The world is talking about eternity. It is high time that the true church of Jesus Christ declares to the world the promises God gives in His Word on how to get to Heaven and how to avoid Hell. The alternative to Hell is the glorious joy that awaits those who will follow Jesus Christ, the Savior of the world, to His heavenly home.

Jesus prayed, "Father, I desire that they also . . . be with Me *where I am*" (John 17:24 NASB).

THE OLD TESTAMENT

CHAPTER 1

TREE OF ETERNAL LIFE

From Beginning to Unending

Behold, the man has become like one of Us, to know good and evil. . . . and take also of the tree of life . . . and live **forever**.

—GENESIS 3:22

THIS IS A PERFECT PLACE TO START—THE BEGINNING. Can you imagine a symphony that plays only the ending of a song? Or a baseball team playing only the last inning?

Has a child ever run up to you, breathlessly telling you only what happened at the end of the story? You stop him or her and say, "Start at the beginning."

Genesis, which means "origin," is the account of how God began His relationship with mankind. And the Author of the beginning does all things perfectly. So God tells us that "in the beginning" He created the heavens and the earth, then made the first man and woman in His image. He showered Adam and Eve with His love and wanted them to return that love willingly.

We know the story. He made creation so beautiful and intended for mankind to enjoy His paradise. He made a home for Adam and Eve where they could walk with God in the cool of the evening. The setting was really more than we can fathom. If we could gather lush tropics, majestic mountains, fruited plains, pristine lakes, mighty oceans, and the splendor of the shorelines all in one place, it could not begin to compare to the grand design of the garden of Eden—it was a little Heaven on earth.

In the midst of this mansion of God's handiwork, shaded by every tree imaginable, stood the tree of life. "God made every tree grow that is pleasant to the sight and good for food. The tree of life was also in the midst of the garden, and the tree of the knowledge of good and evil" (Genesis 2:9). Let's not miss the significance of this verse that describes two trees: the tree of life and the tree of knowledge of good and evil. Here we are introduced to two "paths," which we will follow throughout Scripture.

Genesis is the book of firsts: creation, marriage, family, and fellowship with God. This is also where man heard God's very first command and where we see that God granted man the freedom of choice—to live eternally or die spiritually: "Of every tree of the garden you may freely eat; but of the tree of the knowledge of good and evil you shall not eat, for in the day that you eat of it you shall surely die" (vv. 16–17).

This was a breathtaking message from God, who abundantly gives life. He told the first couple, "Look around. Behold the abundance from My hand. Enjoy all of this beauty. Drink in the wealth that is from above, and eat from the tree of life, which will produce eternal blessings. Enjoy the freedom that is yours forever."

One would think that Adam and Eve would stand in awe of that promise. But we see quickly that their minds, instead, gravitated to God's one very small warning: do not eat of the tree of knowledge of good and evil lest you die. Here they were introduced to the idea of death and the interlude to eternity.

I can remember hearing the story of a father who took his little girl to the park. She was free to slide, swing, and skip through the playground. But her father warned her not to go near a certain bush along the fence. When he turned his back, that's right where she headed, and as a result she found herself covered in poison ivy.

Why is it that we humans just have to defy warnings when they are designed for our own good? The answer comes to us from "the beginning." It is man's sin.

Scripture tells us that the devil said to the woman, "God doesn't mean what He says. You're not going to die. If you eat of the fruit of that tree, you will be as great as God." So, being tempted, Eve ate the first fruit of the forbidden tree and brought some to Adam (see Genesis 3:4–6). This is when the fall of man occurred and rebellion against God took root in the human heart. The entire human race has been suffering and dying since that bitter day long ago.

The original sin was, and still is, the human choice to be one's own god. This is the sin of pride—to control one's own life, to be in charge, not to be accountable to anyone, not even to the One who breathed into the body the very breath of life.

Adam's and Eve's eyes were opened to the difference between good and evil, and the fruit they ate left a very bitter aftertaste, so much so that when God called out to them, they hid.

Sin must be fully judged. Adam and Eve were expelled from the garden, keeping them from the source of eternal life—the tree of life—which represents Christ. They were going to face death. God's Word is His oath, so He drove them out of the garden and placed an angel there to guard the way to the tree of life.

But God did not turn His back on His creation; He had a plan to save the human race. Even from the beginning, He determined to send His Son to this earth. And on the cross, made from the timbers of a tree, Jesus died for man's sin and reconciled him to God in Heaven. The cross became the symbol of sacrifice; the tree became the symbol of life eternal.

Do you think about death and what follows? Most of us think about where we want to live, if we have health insurance, and what our retirement plan is, but seldom do we plan for death—the gateway to eternity.

When I was preaching this message in Memphis, Tennessee, in 1978, just months after Elvis Presley died, a number of major articles were published about death. *Newsweek* even featured a cover story that May titled "Living with Dying." Think about it: from the moment we are born, we begin to die.

The belief in the immortality of the soul is intuitive and instinctive. When Charlemagne's tomb was opened, all that was left was a jumble of moldy bones; his crown and scepter lay buried in the dust of his tomb. Powerless!

The Taj Mahal holds the remains of a Mogul emperor and his favorite wife. The building itself is glorious, but as for the occupants? No more glory!

Greek philosophers chased after immortality with an intellectual fervor. No nonbeliever in the true God yearned more fervently for a pleasant eternity than Plato, who constantly felt the "longing after immortality."[1] It has also been observed that Aristotle reflected that the "species of mankind possesses immortality."[2] Shakespeare wrote, "I have immortal longings in me."[3] They died and were buried. No more wisdom!

Ancient Egyptians built pyramids for their dead and filled them with provisions for life beyond the grave. An African chief was buried with his wife to give him companionship in the future life. The Norsemen buried horses and armor with their warriors so that they might fight in the afterlife. All these careful provisions still lay moldering—or they've been excavated by archeologists, unused.

Muslims from an earlier day heckled Christian missionaries, saying, "We have the tomb of our great prophet Mohammed here in Medina, while you Christians have nothing."[4] Oh, but we have an empty tomb, for the eternal, immortal One who possesses all power, all glory, and all wisdom is the Life-giver Himself and is not dead—He lives!

Man's heart is consumed with the mystery and terror of continued life after death. It is a universal phenomenon. Yet few make the conscious choice of where they will spend eternity, even though it is their choice to make.

When Jesus died on the cross, He conquered death through His resurrection. There is no reason to fear eternity if you place your trust and faith wholly in the eternal One. The Bible tells us that before the beginning of time, God planned to show the grace of Jesus Christ through the Gospel that shows us the way to life and immortality. The risen Christ became "the firstfruits of those who have fallen asleep" (1 Corinthians 15:20). He holds the keys to death.

Throughout Scripture the Lord spoke through the patriarchs, prophets, and apostles and answered the ancient question from the book of Job: "If a man dies, shall he live again?" (14:14).

Yes indeed.

Both the Old and New Testaments teach life after death. Abraham looked for a city "whose builder and maker is God" (Hebrews 11:10). Peter declared, "For Christ also suffered once for sins, the just for the unjust, that He might bring us to God" (1 Peter 3:18). But it's all there from the start, in Genesis. Throughout this book of beginnings we see life and death, warnings and judgments, God's grace and promises—and God's love for His creation. People down through the centuries have been on the search for love while scoffing at the greatest love story ever demonstrated—that God sent His Son to rescue the human race.

Noah warned of the judgment coming in the form of a flood. But the people refused to listen, and death came to all except Noah and his family. Even in this, God set His rainbow in the cloud as an everlasting promise that He would never again destroy mankind by water.

God made a promise to Abraham that He would be the father of many nations, and the Bible reveals that Abraham believed God and served Him and worshiped Him as the everlasting God. The story was the same for a procession of Abraham's descendants: Isaac, Jacob, Joseph—our ancestors in faith. They struggled at times, but they chose to believe and follow God. And God kept His promises to them.

The God of beginnings and eternal life—the never-endings—still gives us the freedom to choose whether we will live for Him or die in our sins. This is the message I have preached for more than seventy years, inviting people to be reconciled to the Savior, for if we reject Him here, He will reject us on the Day of Judgment.

The invitation that God initiated in the book of beginnings is the same invitation that Christ extends to you at the end of the Scripture: Obey Me. Eat of the tree of life, and be saved forever.

> To him who overcomes I will give to eat from the tree of life,
> which is in the midst of the Paradise of God. (Revelation 2:7)

CHAPTER 2

ETERNAL DELIVERANCE

Deliverance or Defiance

EXODUS

> *In your might, you [deliver] them*
>   *to your sacred home.*
>   *The place, O LORD, reserved for your own*
>   *dwelling . . .*
>   *that your hands have established. . . .*
> **forever and ever.**

—EXODUS 15:13, 17–18 NLT

THE BUSH WAS ABLAZE WITH FIRE, BUT IT DID NOT BURN UP. And when the Lord saw the shepherd approaching, He spoke his name from the burning bush:

"Moses, Moses!"

"Here I am," he replied (Exodus 3:4).

The Lord told Moses that He had heard the cries of distress and suffering from the Israelites and had come down to "deliver them out of the hand of the Egyptians, and to bring them . . . to a land flowing with milk and honey" (v. 8). The Lord tapped Moses on the shoulder and commissioned him to be His spokesman.

As the bush blazed, Moses told the Lord that the people would want to know who sent him. They will ask, "What is His name?" (v. 13).

God replied, "I AM WHO I AM. . . . Thus you shall say to the children of Israel, 'I AM has sent me to you'" (v. 14).

This is a remarkable conversation and one that reveals the awesome and definitive name of God from the Old Testament, "I AM." Jesus used this very name when He was being questioned by the contentious Pharisees.

They asked Jesus, "Where is your Father?"

Jesus answered, "Since you don't know who I am, you don't know who my Father is. If you knew me, you would also know my Father" (John 8:19 NLT).

Their minds were already perplexed because Jesus had said He had come to set the captives free and that He was going away. But many did not believe they needed to be delivered from sin. They simply did not believe He was the promised Messiah, so He told them that they did not belong to God: "You belong to this world; I do not. . . . Unless you believe that I AM who I claim to be, you will die in your sins" (vv. 23–24 NLT).

The Pharisees said, "Are you greater than our father Abraham? He died, and so did the prophets. Who do you think you are?" (v. 53 NLT).

Jesus answered, "I tell you the truth, before Abraham was even born, I AM!" (v. 58 NLT).

The Pharisees understood this language from the Book of the Law, and it made them bristle to think that anyone dared to call Himself by the name of God.

But the great I AM stood before them in truth. Jesus was willing to deliver the Jewish leaders from their self-righteousness and unbelief, but they rejected Him as their Deliverer, just as the children of Israel had rejected almighty God as their King, who had shown His strength and power.

Remember the story of the great exodus, when the Israelites fled Egypt. "And Moses said to the people, 'Do not be afraid. Stand still, and see the salvation of the LORD, which He will accomplish for you today'" (Exodus 14:13). As the Lord held back the water, the great host of people crossed the sea safely on dry ground, saving them from death.

This miracle pointed to what would take place thousands of years later, when salvation's plan was fulfilled in the Land of Promise. When Jesus stretched out His arms on the bloodstained cross, making Himself the Bridge between humanity and God, He secured eternal salvation for all who would come to Him.

> The LORD is my rock and my fortress and my
>   deliverer . . .
> My shield and the horn of my salvation. (Psalm 18:2)

Jesus is not only the eternal Deliverer, but He is the eternal Sustainer. He provides for those who receive Him. Just as God had provided daily manna from Heaven to the children of Israel on their wilderness journey, so Jesus provides for the soul-hunger of people today. He was born in Bethlehem, which literally means "house of bread," and proclaimed, "I am the living bread which came down from heaven. If anyone eats of this bread, he will live forever" (John 6:51).

Jesus is also the everlasting Guide. The Lord led the Israelites through the Sinai Desert during the day with a pillar of cloud, and He provided light at night with a pillar of fire. Jesus said, "I am the light of the world. He who follows Me shall not walk in darkness, but have the light of life" (8:12).

Scientists really don't know what light is, but we all know its many effects. We know that there could be no plant, animal, or human life upon the earth without light.

God put the sun in precise balance and distance from the earth. If it were a few miles closer, we would be burned up. If it were a farther distance from the earth, we would freeze. What the sun is to the earth,

Jesus Christ is to the spiritual world. What effect the sun has on nature is the effect Jesus has on our cold, lifeless, and sinful natures. Christ wants to turn His light on in our hearts. He wants us to be reflectors of His divine Light.

I have traveled to every continent in the world and have been a witness to the difference God's light makes in the people who possess Him. We are His light in a dark world.

The world today is steeped in immorality and threatened by terrorism. But we also have extraordinary doors open to us for the Gospel. "See, I have set before you an open door, and no one can shut it; for you have . . . kept My word, and have not denied My name" (Revelation 3:8).

Every nation has points of entry, just as the children of Israel did when they crossed the Jordan River into the Promised Land. God had delivered them out of slavery and persecution into a better country. As Jesus walked the Bible lands, He proclaimed, "I am the door. If anyone enters by Me, he will be saved" (John 10:9).

Every house and building has at least one entrance. The kingdom of God also has an entrance—only one—and it is Jesus Christ, the Door. The human heart has an entrance as well, but many have it bolted, defiantly refusing to let Christ come in. The Bible says, "Behold, I stand at the door and knock. If anyone hears My voice and opens the door, I will come in to him" (Revelation 3:20).

Think of how many doors Jesus probably built while He worked in Joseph's carpenter shop. He also formed our hearts and wants to dwell there, but many have locked theirs up and thrown away the key.

In 1971, when the crew of *Apollo 15* returned to the earth's atmosphere after a journey of nearly three hundred hours and almost half a million miles, they had to reenter the earth's atmosphere through a corridor less than forty miles wide. That is a narrow passage. This illustrates what Jesus said: "Enter by the narrow gate; for wide is the gate and broad is the way that leads to destruction. . . . Narrow is the gate and difficult is the way which leads to life, and there are few who find it" (Matthew 7:13–14).

This "life" is found only in Jesus, who said, "I am the true vine. . . . Every branch in Me that does not bear fruit He takes away; and every branch that bears fruit He prunes, that it may bear more fruit" (John 15:1–2). The olive branch has become a symbol for the Jewish people, and it was an olive leaf that the dove brought back to Noah after the Flood as the sign of life. In the Gospel of John, Jesus speaks of the branches, foreshadowing eternity and distinguishing between those who genuinely follow Him to Heaven eternal and those who follow their father the devil into Hell everlasting.

But Jesus continues to call people to Him, just as the shepherds call their sheep and their sheep know them. Jesus said, "I am the good shepherd" (John 10:11). "My Presence will go with you" (Exodus 33:14).

Sheep rarely last long without a shepherd. They easily fall prey to wolves. They wander and become hopelessly lost, and they cannot see twenty feet beyond their noses. Isn't this a picture of mankind—a straying flock that possesses similar characteristics? Sheep need a deliverer. Jesus is our eternal Deliverer. The Bible says that our spiritual eyesight is faulty. The prophet Isaiah wrote,

> All we like sheep have gone astray;
> We have turned, every one, to his own way. (Isaiah 53:6)

Shepherds in the Middle East provide for and protect their sheep, but Jesus gave His very life for His sheep. We are helpless without Him. And it is through His life that we have hope and assurance for life ever after. Jesus said, "I am the resurrection and the life. He who believes in Me, though he may die, he shall live" (John 11:25).

Every day should be lived with eternity on our minds. If we did this, we would live differently, with purpose and resolve to please the eternal One who is Bread and Light and Vine and Shepherd. The eternal Deliverer, the ever-present I AM, asks this question: "Do you believe this?" (v. 26).

This was the message the apostle Paul preached: "The Lord will deliver me from every evil work and preserve me for His heavenly kingdom. To Him be glory forever and ever" (2 Timothy 4:18). In eternity we will know the everlasting deliverance of our God.

"The Deliverer will come . . .
[and] take away their sins." (Romans 11:26–27)

CHAPTER 3

ONE ETERNAL SACRIFICE

The Gift of the Blood

LEVITICUS, NUMBERS

Whether a native of your own country or a
stranger who dwells among you. . . . this shall be
an **everlasting** *statute for you, to make atonement*
for . . . sins.

—LEVITICUS 16:29, 34

And it shall be to him and his descendants after
him a covenant of an **everlasting** *priesthood,*
because he was zealous for his God, and made
atonement for the children of Israel.

—NUMBERS 25:13

SCIENCE IS LEARNING TO CONTROL JUST ABOUT EVERYTHING BUT
MAN. More important than electricity, technology, and medicine are the

issues of the heart. Solve the problems of hate, lust, greed, and prejudice—which produce social strife and ultimately war—and the world would be a different place. Our future is threatened by many dangers, but they all stem from the heart.

Greater than the enemy outside is the enemy within—sin. Every major civilization before us has disintegrated and collapsed from internal forces rather than military conquest. Ancient Rome is the outstanding example of the fall of a mighty civilization. While its disintegration was hastened by foreign invasions, in the opinion of a well-known archaeologist, it collapsed "only after bribery and corruption had been rife for generations."

No matter how advanced its progress, any civilization that neglects its spiritual and moral life is going to disintegrate. This is the history of mankind, and it is our problem still today.

President Theodore Roosevelt said, "When you educate a man in mind and not in morals, you educate a menace to society." We need moral absolutes, but people refuse to live by them.

This was the problem with ancient Israel—and with all peoples of the world, past, present, and future. The Bible says that the human heart is corrupt. This is why Christ came—to give new hearts to the human race. Scripture reveals the price required for man's sin. The Israelites were taught that sin must be atoned for by the shedding of pure and innocent blood, as recorded in the books of Leviticus and Numbers.

Some feel that these books are difficult to read, but their passages are rich in history and are pertinent today because they point to the future. Nearly every chapter begins with "And the LORD spoke . . ." There is no lack of warning from almighty God. No one could declare innocence about God's commands. He laid down the law and declared judgment if the law was not obeyed. The people had said, "Show us the law and we will follow it"—but they couldn't do it, and neither can we. So God sent His Son to show us the way.

When the children of Israel were on the move across the wilderness, they had before them the tabernacle of God. When they set up camp to allow for rest, the tabernacle was erected and atonement was made for their sins by the shedding of the innocent blood of an unblemished animal. The process was tedious, demanding, and frequent—because of the people's continual sin. They would sin, repent, and go right back to sinning. Does this remind us of our world today?

To make atonement for sin, the priest would offer the slain animals upon the altar in the Holy of Holies. The shedding of blood was a constant reminder of their release from bondage in Egypt, when innocent blood was brushed on the doorpost of each home, signifying that God would withhold the judgment of death. "For it is the blood that makes atonement for the soul" (Leviticus 17:11). The blood showed obedience and honor to the name of God, inviting His protection. The shedding of blood also pointed to the one eternal sacrifice to come.

Israel had been called by the Lord to be a holy nation. They had come out of the pagan Egyptian society where idol worship and immoral living reigned. God forbade them to continue these practices with warnings and judgment: "But if you do not [according to God's commands], then take note, you have sinned against the LORD; and be sure your sin will find you out" (Numbers 32:23). When the Israelites turned away from godlessness, God's blessings were poured out on them. He desired that His special people would live lives that reflected His holy character.

Not only did God protect His own; He also instructed His people to invite others into His protection by recognizing their sin and also making atonement. We see this wonderful phrase, "a stranger who dwells among you" (Leviticus 16:29), and marvel that God in His great love for all people is constantly making provision for them through the gift of blood that cleanses—not just until the next time we sin but forever. We see the wonderful extension of God's law to foreigners: God said, "Native-born Israelites and foreigners are equal before the LORD. . . . The same instructions and regulations will apply both to you and to the foreigners living among you. . . . When you arrive in the land *where I am taking you*" (Numbers 15:15–16, 18 NLT).

When Christ shed His blood, it was the final sacrifice that had eternal implications. No more would people need to make atonement through animal sacrifice. Christ finished it once and for all with His very life. He became the one eternal sacrifice: "But this Man . . . offered one sacrifice for sins forever. . . . He has perfected forever those who are being sanctified" (Hebrews 10:12, 14).

Now people often say, "Christianity and Judaism are bloody religions! Why must they always be talking about blood?" The Bible tells us, "For the life of the flesh is in the blood" (Leviticus 17:11).

I recall seeing a placard while on a visit to the Mayo Clinic: "Give the Gift of Blood." If you or a loved one were in need of blood to sustain life, would you not feel tremendous relief to know that enough blood had been donated and banked for a life-saving transfusion? Physical life has been preserved through this procedure—people giving their own blood to save another.

The blood of Christ provides life and all that sustains life: redemption, remission, cleansing, justification, reconciliation, peace, access, fellowship, and protection from evil and the evil one.

Blood redeems. Blood, not gold, is the world's most valuable commodity. We are "redeemed . . . with the precious blood of Christ" (1 Peter 1:18–19).

Blood cleanses. You can take unrefined sugar and dip it in the blood of animals, and it will bleach the sugar, turning it white. When you invite Christ to come into your life, His blood cleanses you; His blood pumps through your spiritual veins with eternal life. "The blood of Jesus Christ . . . cleanses us from all sin" (1 John 1:7).

Blood justifies. Paul wrote that "while we were yet sinners, Christ died for us" and "justified [us] by his blood" (Romans 5:8–9 KJV). We are justified—as though we had never sinned.

Blood reconciles. Scripture speaks of the Father in Heaven taking pleasure in reconciling man to Himself and bringing "peace through the blood" of His Son's cross (Colossians 1:20).

Blood provides access. The writer of Hebrews explained clearly how Christ's sacrifice replaced the animal sacrifice, no longer sufficient, giving us "full assurance of faith" in the blood that Jesus shed for us (Hebrews 10:19–22) so we now have full access to the Father's throne of grace.

Blood brings fellowship. Salvation is not just saving us from sin but reestablishing the relationship between God and man. Christ's blood has brought us back into fellowship with Him (Ephesians 2:13).

Blood brings protection. No one can come against us without first coming against Christ. "If God is for us, who can be against us? . . . [Nothing can] separate us from the love of God" (Romans 8:31, 39).

This is the heart of the Gospel, and rightly so. The heart is the pump that keeps the blood flowing through the veins and arteries to cleanse the cells and also to infuse the cells with life. Jesus told us that whoever partakes of His blood has eternal life and will be raised up—infused with life—forever (John 6:54).

God stands ready to forgive. He doesn't have to get ready to forgive. We, on the other hand, have to get ready to repent. We stand ready to sin. We are a stubborn people who want to do things our way. But the way to God is through His one-time sacrifice; living for God is through sanctification, day by day.

Do you need a blood transfusion? You don't have to go through the process of finding the right match. The blood of Jesus is the right type of blood. His is the perfect match, and He offers His blood to you.

A CAT scan may reveal a malignancy in the body, but only the blood of Christ can wash away the evil that afflicts our souls. Antibiotics can kill disease, but only the blood of Christ can blot out transgressions. Laser surgery can be used to remove a tumor on the brain, but only the blood of Christ can purge your conscience of its guilt. An aspirin can banish a headache, but only the blood of Christ can heal your heartache.

A great preacher by the name of César Malan was put out of his church in Switzerland in the early 1800s because of his evangelistic zeal. He traveled to the British Isles and led a number of famous people to God. Once while in England, he met a young woman by the name of

Charlotte Elliott. He told her that the greatest news that had ever come into his life was that the blood of Jesus Christ cleansed him from his sin.

Charlotte Elliott, though gifted and attractive, was embittered because of ill health. She said, "I cannot believe in the goodness of God, and I don't need the blood of Jesus Christ to forgive me for anything!"

Malan said, "I didn't mean to be offensive; I only meant to tell you that God loves you and that He has forgiven you at a great cost."

That night Charlotte Elliott could not sleep because of the words the preacher had spoken to her. She finally went to her knees and asked Christ into her heart. Years later she wrote these words:

> Just as I am, without one plea,
> But that Thy blood was shed for me.[1]

Believers in Christ have a fabulous future ahead. Thank Jesus Christ now for the gift of His blood and know that in His dying He gave us the everlasting promise of what one eternal sacrifice would mean—eternal life. Though the present structure of society will someday disappear and all its progress will be wiped out as a result of man's failure and folly, those who believe in Jesus Christ will know the eternal significance of this precious gift of His shed blood.

With His own blood He entered the Most Holy Place once
for all, having obtained eternal redemption. (Hebrews 9:12)

— CHAPTER 4 ——————————————————————

ETERNAL JUDGMENT

Choose Life

DEUTERONOMY

*Those things which are revealed belong to us and
our children* **forever**. . . .
    *I have set before you life and death . . . therefore
choose life.*

—DEUTERONOMY 29:29; 30:19

CHOOSE LIFE. It is a popular phrase these days and is associated with the right-to-life campaign. The slogan was lifted from God's Word and is found in the book of Deuteronomy—from the days when Moses governed the people of Israel.

The Bible places the highest value on human life. It is sacred and of inestimable worth to God, who created life "in His own image" (Genesis 1:27). His creation plan was designed with eternal life in view, which is why He planted the tree of life in the midst of the garden. Then came sin. Then came death.

From that moment, every heartbeat brings man one step closer to death. But in the process of life, God gives us a choice: to choose eternal life or to choose the horrors of outer darkness forever.

Surprisingly, many do not choose life.

This choice hinges on God's first commandment, which is the key to defining sin: "You shall have no other gods before Me" (Exodus 20:3). To break this commandment brings the sentence of death. This is what happened with Adam and Eve. They made a choice—the wrong choice.

There are only two kinds of people: the saved and the unsaved. The Bible is the story of two roads, two choices. Sacrifice or selfishness, salvation or damnation, belief in Jesus or rejection of Him, abundant life or eternal punishment, Heaven or Hell. Regardless of the choice, it will cost something. Making the right choice to live for Jesus, many believers will be ostracized, ridiculed, even persecuted. Some will be rejected by their families and friends. Others will have to conduct business on a higher plane because Christ in us will change us.

I remember a man who was saved during the early part of our 1957 Madison Square Garden crusade. He told me a few weeks later, "Billy, last week I lost twenty-two thousand dollars on a deal because it was a little bit shady. Before my conversion I would have clinched the deal without a thought."

Salvation is free to us, but it cost Jesus His life. It will also cost you your sins if you choose to receive His gift. That does not mean you have to clean up your life before you can be saved. The Lord knows you don't have the power to do that. You must come to Him in repentance, and *then* His Holy Spirit will move in, take up residence in you, and empower you to walk away from sin. That's why Jesus paid for our sins with His blood—to set us on a new path with the Holy Spirit as our daily guide.

Now many people quickly say, "Well, I do love God and follow Him." This is wonderful, but be sure by putting it to the test. Do you prove your love to God when you slander someone? Do you show your love to Him when you cheat or lie or go against His commands? The Bible says, "Now by this we know that we know Him, if we keep His commandments. He who says, 'I know Him,' and does not keep His commandments, is a liar, and the truth is not in him" (1 John 2:3–4).

Can you imagine living in disobedience while claiming the Holy Spirit is guiding you? If you do so without conviction and repentance, you do not love Jesus—because Jesus said His Spirit would convict of sin.

One of the saddest statements in the Bible is when Jesus said, "Not everyone who says to Me, 'Lord, Lord,' shall enter the kingdom of heaven. . . . Many will say to Me in that day, 'Lord, Lord, have we not . . . done many wonders in Your name?' And then I will declare to them, 'I never knew you; depart from Me, you who practice lawlessness!'" (Matthew 7:21–23).

There will be no dodging, no whimpering, no whining, nor crying in hopes that He will change His mind. The Lord will not acknowledge what man claims to believe but what he actually believes and puts into action.

Choose this day the road to travel into eternity. Don't think there are three choices—yes, no, and wait—for you may never have another opportunity. The Bible is the book of two pathways. But only one leads to life eternal.

You may think you are on the right road, but you may be going the wrong way. I remember a famous story of the 1929 Rose Bowl, where an incredibly talented football player named Roy Riegels picked up a fumble and ran sixty-four yards while seventy thousand people cheered him on. He was determined to win the game for the team. Instead, he ran the wrong way to a miserable defeat.

You have to know what you believe and why you believe it before you can know where you are going.

So you ask, "What must I do?" Say yes to Christ. It involves a choice of your intellect. It is a choice of your emotions. It is a choice of your will. It must be a choice of your total personality, yielded to Christ by faith in Him.

You may think because you've been in church all your life that you are on the right road. But that could be the broadest road of all if you are there for the wrong reason. Church membership does not save. I remember preaching in a large Southern city years ago during a political campaign. A prominent man was running for governor, and he joined a church because he said it would help him with the voters. Perhaps it did, but it won't help him with God.

Others may say, "Well, Billy, I have done great works. I am a moral person. I've lived a good life and have treated my neighbor well. Isn't that enough?" No. Don't think that just because you feed people and give money to the needy, you will earn eternal life. That misconception is a trick of Satan's, and it will bring about God's eternal judgment.

Too often we are guilty of building a Christian faith according to our ideas rather than according to the revealed Word of God. We want to picture Christ as soft and pliable, a friend to everyone, someone to hang around with.

Let me tell you what the Bible says, for one day we will see Jesus in all of His glory. "His eyes [were] like a flame of fire; His feet were like fine brass. . . . Out of His mouth went a sharp two-edged sword, and His countenance was like the sun shining in its strength" (Revelation 1:14–16). Quite a different picture, isn't it?

Strange as it may seem, God's judgment is based on His love, and His wrath and righteousness are pure and holy. When the Lord "descended in the cloud" to proclaim Himself to Moses, He said of Himself "The LORD God, merciful and gracious . . . abounding in goodness and truth, keeping mercy . . . forgiving iniquity . . . by no means clearing the guilty" (Exodus 34:5–7). The only way to be freed from the guilt of sin—and God's wrath—is to be reconciled to Him through Jesus Christ.

One of the most neglected Bible doctrines of our time is God's judgment. Some say there is a difference in the wrath of God of the Old Testament and the wrath of God of the New Testament. I find no such thing in my study of Scripture.

Paul wrote specifically about this:

For the wrath of God is revealed from heaven against all un-godliness and unrighteousness of men, who suppress the truth in unrighteousness, because what may be known of God is manifest in them, for God has shown it to them. For since the creation of the world His invisible attributes are clearly seen . . . even His eternal power . . . so that [unbelievers] are without excuse. (Romans 1:18–20)

But all those who have received Christ's full pardon are assured of eternal forgiveness. Abraham said to God, "Far be it from You . . . to slay the righteous with the wicked, so that the righteous should be as the wicked. . . . Shall not the Judge of all the earth do right?" (Genesis 18:25). Yes, indeed. The Lord does all things perfectly well.

God has never executed judgment without giving fair warning; yet we read about the people of Israel complaining about God to the prophet Ezekiel, claiming that His way was unfair. God answered, "It is their way which is not fair! When the righteous turns from his righteousness and commits iniquity, he shall die because of it. But when the wicked turns from his wickedness and does what is lawful and right, he shall live. . . . I will judge every one of you according to his own ways" (Ezekiel 33:17–20). There is nothing more fair than this. He is the rightful judge.

Even with accusations hurled at God, He never changes. In spite of man's continual sin, the grace and patience of the Lord is overwhelming. You can't miss the countless warnings and the pleas that come from God: "'As I live,' says the Lord GOD, 'I have no pleasure in the death of the wicked, but that the wicked turn from his way and live. Turn, turn from your evil ways! For why should you die?'" (v. 11).

Unless we allow Christ to destroy the evil within us, the evil within us still wants to destroy Him. This is the conflict of the ages.

Many people refuse to turn from sin because they are more afraid of man's ridicule than of God's judgment. Others think belief in Christ is foolishness. Well, let's see who is foolish. The whole world laughed at Noah when he boarded an ark on dry land. Lot's neighbors in Sodom and Gomorrah laughed when he ran from the cities, saying they would be destroyed because of rampant immorality. But these eternal judgments were fulfilled as scoffers drowned in the Flood and burned in the brimstone. "'The LORD will judge . . .' It is a fearful thing to fall into the hands of the living God" (Hebrews 10:30–31).

A greater judgment than these took place more than two thousand years ago on Mount Calvary, when the sins of the world were placed on Jesus. He shed His blood on the cross to pay the penalty for sin. Who are we to say that God has no right to judge us? He already has. But the sentence has not been put into motion.

"The Lord knows those who are His," the Bible reminds us. "Let everyone who names the name of Christ depart from iniquity" (2 Timothy 2:19). And why? Because the Bible tells us that Jesus "will judge the living and the dead at His appearing and His kingdom" (4:1).

Plato, the ancient Greek philosopher, said that the soul is always drawn to its judge. He reasoned that humans know instinctively that they will one day stand in resurrected form before God. People do not like to think of God in terms of judgment. But such an attitude is idolatry, an attempt to make God in our own image, as though we are the ones who are right. The Lord knows the heart of men, and nothing is hidden from Him (Luke 12:2).

People bristle at the idea of God's wrath, as though He has no right to judge. If you were going before a judge to settle a dispute with someone who wronged you and the judge decided in your favor, you would praise the judge and believe that justice was done, even for the one who was wrong. God is the Holy and Just One, and His judgments will be perfectly executed.

These truths are hard, but they are necessary. We love to talk about God's Heaven, but are reluctant to mention God's judgment seat. The whole Gospel is not proclaimed until God's warning is given. The apostle Paul said that he had not held anything back in declaring the "whole counsel of God" (Acts 20:27). After he preached to the Corinthians that all will appear before the judgment seat of Christ, he said, "Knowing, therefore, the terror of the Lord, we persuade men" (2 Corinthians 5:11).

This is a dramatic picture of the eternal judgment of God. "Eternal" means it will happen, it will come to pass, it will be executed, and it will be forever. God has set the unchangeable date. The entire human race will stand before Him. He is God, and He will keep His word.

We are all accustomed to changing or breaking appointments, but this is one we will all keep. The Lord is going to open the Book of Life. For those whose names are not found there, it will be because of their unbelief.

I don't want to be judged by an angel who never shed a tear. I don't want to be judged by seraphim who never felt pain. I don't want to be judged by a cherub who never knew human grief or disappointment. I will be judged by the Lamb of God, who became flesh and dwelt among us to identify with our suffering. He is the only One worthy to judge our standing with Him.

No one deserves God's love, but He offers it anyway. His saving grace changes our course from eternal judgment to life eternal. Choose life.

He who believes in the Son has everlasting life; and
he who does not believe the Son shall not see life, but
the wrath of God abides on him. (John 3:36)

POWER FOREVER

Choose or Lose —

JOSHUA

Know that the LORD's hand is powerful . . .
forever.

—JOSHUA 4:24 NLT

"CHIANG KAI-SHEK HAS DIED." When I heard that news on April 5, 1975, I went to my study and closed the door to pray and meditate. The death of the president of the Republic of China brought sadness. It seemed as though the whole extraordinary life of this legendary leader passed in review.

Under his powerful leadership, China had united for the first time in a century. He served as the nation's leader for twenty-one years.

There is warmth in my heart for China because it is where my wife, Ruth, was born and reared. Her father, Dr. L. Nelson Bell, went to China in 1916 as a medical missionary. During his years there he met and came to admire Generalissimo Chiang Kai-shek and later Madame Chiang, one of the world's most intelligent and beautiful women. The general's marriage to Soong Mei-ling was a storybook romance, and she captivated the American people when, during World War II, she addressed a joint session of the United States Congress.

After years of battles, dissensions, and difficulties that plagued all the countries involved in a long war, he was forced to leave his beloved mainland—now under Communist rule. He established a government in exile on the beautiful but poverty-stricken island of Taiwan and turned it into an economic and political stronghold.

My first meeting with Generalissimo Chiang was in 1952. The Korean War was in progress, and I had gone to spend Christmas with the American troops. After I left Korea, I went to Taipei to visit missionaries, preach to the Christians, and visit the hospitals. While there, I unexpectedly received an invitation to dinner from President and Madame Chiang Kai-shek. I was amazed that during that visit almost the entire conversation centered on Christianity.

I was honored, years later, to speak at President Chiang Kai-shek's memorial service, held at the Washington Cathedral, and give some perspective on his personal Christian faith. Close friends in whom I have confidence had shared with me their many experiences with President Chiang.

I learned that Soong Mei-ling had not wished to marry Chiang Kai-shek until he became a Christian. While he was courting her, her godly mother was deeply concerned. She sought the help of her pastor to pray with her, and she gave the general a Bible to read. At that time he was fighting against the warlords in the north of China. In the weeks that followed, he was caught up in a difficult military situation. In desperation he called on the "Christian God" of whom he had been reading and told God that if he was delivered and his life spared, he would publicly confess Christ. True to his promise, he came to his moment of decision, publicly professed his faith in Christ, and was baptized in 1933. The life that followed, in devotion to the Lord Jesus, was a demonstration of the reality of his faith by the power of Christ.

When the general arrived in Taiwan, he erected a small brick chapel close to his home. Christian worship was observed there every Sunday, and he invited members of his governmental staff and a few guests to worship with him. But this was never publicized in the press. The chapel was a place for sincere worship by President and Madame Chiang and their friends.

Chiang was unashamed of his faith. For years it was his custom to go on nationwide radio every Christmas Eve to give a message on the significance of the birth of Jesus Christ. On Good Friday, he customarily delivered a sermon in his private chapel for those who gathered there. A close friend of mine attended on several occasions and was always thrilled at the generalissimo's superb messages on the meaning of the cross of Christ.

When Christian missionaries fled the mainland to Taiwan, the president opened the door of the entire nation to them. As a result, Christian churches flourished across Taiwan. God uses men and women to do His work.

But one of the most important decisions the generalissimo made concerning Christianity was in 1951. Leaders of the Pocket Testament League, an American organization, visited President Chiang in his office and asked permission to distribute Bibles to his army. He voluntarily issued a statement that was publicized throughout the army and throughout Taiwan. In it he stated,

> [It always gives me] pleasure to have people read and study the Bible, since the Bible is the Voice of the Holy Spirit. It reveals the righteousness of God and His love. Jesus Christ our Redeemer gave His life and shed His blood to save those who believe in Him. His righteousness exalts the nation. Christ is the Cornerstone of all freedoms. His love covers all sins; all who believe in Him shall have eternal life.[1]

This man was powerful in his witness for Christ and became a man of the Bible. Following his conversion, it was his lifetime habit to read the Bible on his knees every morning. Generalissimo Chiang was also a man of prayer. And it is public knowledge that just a few hours before the president died, he called together his wife, his son, and five or six of the leading officials of the government, including the new president. He spoke to them about his last wishes; it was his verbal testament to his successors. The first words they heard from his lips, soon to be silenced, were "Jesus Christ." He told them, "My Christian faith I have never departed from."

If the generalissimo were to speak for himself today, I think I know what he might say. He would remember the apostle Paul during the last days of his life, for there were similarities in their two lives before they came to Christ.

Before Paul met the Lord on the road to Damascus, he was a man of terror. But his encounter with Jesus Christ dramatically changed him. He did an about-face. One day Paul was on a mission to arrest people because of their faith in Jesus; the next, he was imprisoned for preaching Christ.

When Paul was chained in the Mamertine Dungeon in Rome, awaiting the executioner's final blow, he wrote a letter to the young Timothy; it was his last will and testament. I think the generalissimo would have joined Paul in one part of the letter that speaks of the imperishable witness of his own life. He would have said, as Paul did, "I have fought a good fight, I have finished my course, I have kept the faith" (2 Timothy 4:7 KJV).

Just as the power of God's Word creates everything out of nothing, just as the power of His breath brings life to the soul, so the power of His Word transforms hearts. "He rules by His power forever" (Psalm 66:7).

We see this demonstrated in the life of Joshua, a powerful young man who served Moses on the journey to the Promised Land. He became one of the great military captains—and later a general—in Israel's army. He was obedient, courageous, and faithful. Above all, he was a man of decision and action. Following the death of Moses, God Himself gave General Joshua his orders:

> Moses my servant is dead. Therefore, the time has come for you
> to lead these people. . . . Be strong and very courageous. Be careful
> to obey all the instructions Moses gave you. Do not deviate from

them. . . . Study this Book of Instruction continually. Meditate on it day and night so you will be sure to obey everything written in it. . . . This is my command. (Joshua 1:2, 7–9 NLT)

So Joshua led the multitude of people into the land that God had promised. When they came near to Jericho, he lifted his eyes and saw a Man standing opposite him, with a sword in His hand, who said, "As Commander of the army of the LORD I have now come" (5:14). Joshua was standing before the Lord Himself.

Joshua led the charge against the city of Jericho, and by God's power the city was destroyed. Only a handful who had believed in Him and helped Israel were saved.

In all the victories that Joshua had, he never failed to praise the Commander and the Captain of salvation, saying, "[God] did this so all the nations of the earth might know that the LORD's hand is powerful . . . forever" (4:24 NLT).

But it didn't take long for the Israelites to forget what God had done for them. Joshua found himself standing before the people, pleading with them to repent and turn back to God. His rallying cry before he died was this: "Choose for yourselves this day whom you will serve" (24:15). Joshua told them that regardless of their decision, he was going to serve the Lord forever.

Forever. That's another word for eternity—the never-ending state. Generalissimo Chiang spoke of eternity, and here we see General Joshua reminding those in his command that God's power and might will save forever. As he reminded the Israelites, so must we remember that our reverence to almighty God will live forever in His sight, on earth and in Heaven.

The Lord has testified of His own promises to those who trust Him. What is your last will and testament to those whose lives you influence? What will you be remembered for when your days on earth end? If your heart has been captured by Christ and your lips declare that you believe in the Lord's powerful and mighty salvation, you will live in His everlasting presence.

There is no limit to God. Paul wrote that "His . . . attributes are clearly seen . . . even His eternal power" (Romans 1:20).

There is no limit to God's wisdom. Jude proclaimed,

> To God our Savior,
> Who alone is wise,
> Be glory and majesty,
> Dominion and power,
> Both now and forever. (Jude 25)

There is no limit to His power. The psalmist declared,

> God has spoken once . . .
> That power belongs to God. (Psalm 62:11)

There is no limit to His glory and love for mankind: "But we see Jesus . . . crowned with glory and honor. . . . For it was fitting for Him . . . in bringing many sons to glory, to make the captain of their salvation perfect through sufferings" (Hebrews 2:9–10).

He saves those who come to Him in their weakness. We don't have to lose in this life; we can choose to win and gain eternity in Heaven. He will empower us to live for Him. "For though He was crucified in weakness, yet He lives by the power of God. For we also are weak in Him, but we shall live with Him by the power of God" (2 Corinthians 13:4). He makes it possible for a weak and sinful heart to melt by the truth of His Word and find redemption.

> The everlasting God. . . .
> Gives power to the weak,
> And to those who have no might He increases
> strength. (Isaiah 40:28–29)

CHAPTER 6

ETERNAL JUDGE— ETERNAL REDEEMER

Strong and Rebellious—Submissive and Secure

JUDGES, RUTH

May the LORD, the Judge, render judgment this day.

—JUDGES 11:27

You redeem my right of redemption for yourself, for I cannot redeem it.

—RUTH 4:6

TWO CONTRASTING STORIES: THE ICONIC STRONGMAN SAMSON AND THE BEAUTIFUL FOREIGNER NAMED RUTH. (Perhaps you were expecting the name *Delilah*, but her story would not be a contrast to Samson at all, for they were both self-serving.) These stories fall between those of Joshua, the leader who entered the Promised Land with the wandering Israelites, and their first king, Saul, who ruled the kingdom.

35

The book of Judges is dark and sobering. It covers perhaps the most degrading period in the history of God's people. God, the eternal Judge, raised up twelve judges to rule over the people, who had gone astray. They had been told to drive out the evil occupants of the Promised Land, but the people had done just the opposite and mingled with pagan society, adopting the ways of their enemy.

Anything contrary to God's Word is the enemy. The children of Israel had been called to a higher plane. They belonged to God and were to be living examples of the freedom and protection He provided.

The beginning and ending of the story are the same: "everyone did what was right in his own eyes" (Judges 21:25)—and what they saw as right was often wrong and evil (2:11). People disregarded God's commands. They diverted from God's way and went their own way. They chose to forget the God who delivered them from slavery, homelessness, hunger, thirst, and discouragement. Instead of driving the enemy out of their land as God commanded, they moved in with them, though God warned against it.

Our present society isn't much different. Too many people today feel that the old moral standards are useless and out of date. They believe they ought to be free to make up their own minds about what is right and wrong, thus doing what is right in their own eyes.

Worldly thinking is, "If you expect to get ahead in life, you'll need to adapt to worldly living and learn to fit in." That's where compromise slips in—that little voice that urges you to lighten up, to give in, whispering that it's okay to go along in insignificant acts. But this is the voice of temptation that comes from the devil. Take the dreadful four-letter word *evil*, add a *d*, and you have discovered Satan's DNA and where he desires to lead you—into evil.

You have heard the saying, "The devil is in the details." Well, Solomon wrote that it is "the little foxes that spoil the vines" (Song of Solomon 2:15). If we do not pay attention to the little things that distract us, we will find ourselves in the midst of a big thing that will undo us. We're no different from those ancient people. We convince ourselves that there is no such thing as right or wrong, that we should be free to decide how we want to behave. But the Bible is very clear about right and wrong.

When we settle for status quo, we've settled for defeat when God has called us to victory. We excuse our bad habits, trying to convince ourselves and others that bad isn't so bad. Habits become unbreakable, unbendable, so our wills refuse to bend to God's. When that happens, He has no choice but to break us—judge us. This was the case with Samson.

The Bible never covers up sin but exposes it. Few men had been given greater opportunity than Samson. He was raised up by God to be strong, but he literally collapsed because he was rebellious. He made the wrong choices and did the wrong things. He exchanged his potential and power for selfishness and weakness.

Samson had been raised in a godly home by parents who revered God and taught Samson to do the same. But he abused God's blessings and became arrogant and disrespectful; he lived a shameful life. In his youth he determined that his parents were out of touch with society. He had been born to stand alone and be used of God, but he wanted to fit in. He didn't take the eternal God seriously. He reflected what so many say today—that the Gospel is out of style and has no relevance. Rubbish!

Samson's life mirrored the life of his nation. He left home in search of excitement and was lured by worldly ways. I can remember as a boy deciding to leave home. I am glad that I never got farther than two blocks. Home is a mighty safe place to be.

Samson was strong physically but weak in every other way. He broke the first commandment, to put God first in everything. Instead, he put himself first and ignored God's rules. Samson broke the second and fifth commandments and worshiped the shrine of lust by taking a Philistine wife against his parents' wishes. He broke the sixth commandment and murdered. He broke the ninth and tenth commandments because he lied and coveted (Judges 13–16).

We look at Samson's life and can see ourselves in the mirror. We make life-changing choices for good or bad. When we choose the bad, it is because the seed of sin is within us. It can only be rooted out by salvation in Jesus Christ.

"To whom much is given," the Bible says, ". . . much [is] required" (Luke 12:48). This was Samson's profile; he had been given everything life had to offer. But instead of treasuring it and being responsible with it, he decided to "live it up." Samson was bored, and boredom often leads to discouragement or, as in the case of young Samson, mischief. He chased after whatever pleased him and was headed for a catastrophic fall. When he let his guard down, he was bound up by the enemy.

Seduced by Delilah, he divulged to her the secret of his strength. The enemy swooped in and took him prisoner. His eyes, which had lusted after beautiful Delilah, were gouged out, and he was forced to grind millstones. The Samson who had once boasted of his strength and easy lifestyle was now pitifully blind, bound in bronze chains, and forced into monotonous slave labor grinding grain. The very people he had chased after now mocked him for their amusement as they watched him circle the grinding mill hours a day.

It is true that God empowered Samson one last time to bring judgment down on His enemies. But Samson went down with them, dying a horrible and violent death. This is a wrenching story. And whatever victory came out of Samson's life came from God's hand alone.

The world will offer kicks, thrills, and blasts. Beware, though; such allurement will bring you down! Don't be strongheaded and weak like Samson. The Bible tells us to be strong in the Lord and in the power of His might. You may have to stand alone in school. You may have to stand alone in college. You may have to stand alone at work. You may have to stand alone in life—but stand alone and live a clean and decent life. The pent-up energy that comes with youth can be a beacon of light for the Lord Jesus Christ, or it can turn your world into a dark and dingy place, as in the days of the judges. Dedicate your energies to the Lord.

This is certainly what young Ruth did. Her story of love and devotion stands in stark contrast to Samson's dark tale. Ruth's mother-in-law, Naomi, found herself widowed in the foreign land of Moab. Her sons had married Moabites but had both died young, leaving Naomi with two daughters-in-law, Orpah and Ruth.

Naomi decided to return home to Israel and tried to persuade the young widows to remain in their homeland and remarry. Orpah did, but Ruth pleaded to go with Naomi, saying,

> Wherever you go, I will go;
> And wherever you lodge, I will lodge;
> Your people shall be my people,
> And your God, my God.
> Where you die, I will die,
> And there will I be buried. (Ruth 1:16–17)

Ruth was willing to walk away from her homeland, her idol worship, and her way of life, and join with her mother-in-law, embracing her strong faith. No in-law story could be as precious as this. What Ruth saw in Naomi drew her to the Lord, and she submitted herself and found security in Him.

I suppose I have always been drawn to this love story because my late wife's name was Ruth. But the story also pulls me in because it is a picture of God's great desire to be loved by His people. The Lord did something very wonderful in Ruth's life and the life of Boaz, Naomi's kinsman, who married Ruth and redeemed her heritage. He became a glorious picture of the eternal Redeemer who was to come.

God blessed Ruth and Boaz by giving them a son named Obed, who had a son named Jesse, who became the father of King David. We cannot miss the eternal significance, knowing that Jesus was born in the line of David.

> For His mercy endures forever.
> Let the redeemed of the LORD say so,
> Whom He has redeemed from the hand of the enemy. (Psalm 107:1–2)

CHAPTER 7

ETERNAL KING, ETERNAL THRONE, ETERNAL KINGDOM

Manpower or God's Power

1 AND 2 SAMUEL, 1 AND 2 KINGS, 1 AND 2 CHRONICLES

> *He is the tower of salvation to His king . . .*
> **forevermore**.
>
> —2 SAMUEL 22:51

> *The throne of David shall be established before the*
> LORD **forever**. . . . *that all the kingdoms of the earth*
> *may know that You are the* LORD *God, You alone.*
>
> —1 KINGS 2:45, 2 KINGS 19:19

> *I will establish the throne of his kingdom . . .*
> **forever**.
>
> —1 CHRONICLES 22:10

"THEY HAVE REJECTED ME, THAT I SHOULD NOT REIGN OVER THEM" (1 Samuel 8:7). This is the sordid history of a nation who couldn't be satisfied with the Lord as their King.

God brought Israel through famine and gave them bounty. He brought them through slavery and gave them freedom. He brought them through the wilderness and gave them the Land of Promise. He was their eternal King, but they wanted a human king: "We will have a king over us," they cried, "that we also may be like all the nations" (vv. 19–20).

God finally told the prophet Samuel to heed their voice and give them what they desired. "However," God told Samuel, "you shall solemnly forewarn them, and show them the behavior of the king who will reign over them" (v. 9).

The prophet declared that a king of the flesh would disappoint them, but Israel would not listen. All the more they cried for a king who would "judge us and go out before us and fight our battles" (v. 20). They were shortsighted. How could they so quickly forget the miracles that God performed before their eyes? Victory over Pharaoh. Protection of their firstborns from the royal sword. Deliverance from the Egyptian army through the Red Sea. Manna from Heaven and water from the rock in the wilderness. Battles won and nations conquered as they seized the Land of Promise. God had given Israel His power, wisdom, protection, and love. But no, Israel wanted an ordinary king like the other nations.

When the mind is on the flesh, it thinks small. We see this today. Our country has been richly blessed of God, yet many are dissatisfied and cry out to be like other nations. Unimaginable, but not unordinary. The human race simply cannot be content. Why? It is because the heart runs after the things of the world, which fail to satisfy; so the chase will continue until the end of time. "For all that is in the world—the lust of the flesh, the lust of the eyes, and the pride of life—is not of the Father but is of the world. . . . But he who does the will of God abides forever" (1 John 2:16–17).

In these six Old Testament books a light shines on the agonizing history of Israel's kings and kingdoms. Yet God in His sovereignty remained patient and did not turn His back on His people, despite their sinful and selfish hearts. It was not without great price, however, that they exchanged the Lord of Heaven for a mere man to rule over them. Israel was in disarray, corrupted by sin. They had returned to worshiping idols—other gods. They wanted manpower—not God's power!

The New Testament points back to the Old, and the Old Testament scriptures look forward to the new covenant that was foretold. At every turn, God's hand moved on behalf of His people. But out of this weary cycle of sin, repentance, forgiveness, and sin again emerges the faithfulness of God's eternal promises. He turned Israel's deepest sorrow into the nation's greatest hope: from the throne of David would come the promised Messiah, who would establish Israel's throne and kingdom forever.

God exhibited mercy to Israel repeatedly, only to receive rejection. This same mercy was extended to mankind from the cross. He couldn't have opened His arms wider to embrace the dying world, though the nature of man despised and rejected Him.

Before we become too critical of the Israelites, we should ask ourselves if we don't do the same. The Lord has blessed many nations of the world, but none as much as America. Yet our country has turned its back on Him. A call for national and individual repentance is urgently needed today, while His great love still quietly convicts. The Bible says, "Oh, the depth of the riches both of the wisdom and knowledge of God! How unsearchable are His judgments and His ways past finding out" (Romans 11:33).

A familiar passage from the time of the kings reveals the Lord's heart as He responded to a prayer of King Solomon's: "If My people who are called by My name will humble themselves, and pray and seek My face, and turn from their wicked ways, then I will hear from heaven, and will forgive their sin and heal their land" (2 Chronicles 7:14).

While this passage is very specific to the nation of Israel concerning their land, there are many things we can learn from God's plea. God's message is always the same: repent of sin and turn to Me.

It is clear that God's healing was dependent upon the people's obedience to follow His commands. He would bless them, and then they would become complacent or rebellious, falling back into idolatry—something they had learned from their pagan neighbors. We may look at this pattern and say, "Why couldn't they see that?" Because this is the pattern of sin in the human heart: people seek their own way. This pattern is chronicled as occurring again and again. When the people obeyed God, He blessed them. When they disobeyed, He sent judgment. Please do not miss the significance of the fallout from sin. God will forgive, but sin leaves a dreadful mess.

I have heard this passage of God's words to Solomon recited at both religious and secular events and wondered if people really understood. They would so readily agree to "turn from their wicked ways" but then fail to do it. As people, we want what we want, and we want it now.

The *Los Angeles Times* carried an ad that read: "Spend Now—Pay Later!" We are always chasing after what the world says is better. Before we know it, we have exchanged faith in God for following the gods of this world. This is the repetitive history of the human race.

A thought-provoking quotation appeared in the paper around the time of America's two hundredth birthday and has been reprinted several times since then:

The world's great civilizations averaged a cycle of 200 years. Those societies progressed through this sequence:

From bondage to spiritual faith.
From spiritual faith to great courage.
From great courage to liberty.
From liberty to abundance.
From abundance to selfishness.
From selfishness to complacency.
From complacency to apathy.
From apathy to dependency.
From dependency back again into bondage.[1]

On September 11, 2001, the world watched in horror as America was assaulted; two hijacked airplanes crashed into the World Trade Center in New York City, and the buildings collapsed before our eyes. The horrific event brought Americans to their knees—for a few weeks. It threatened our national pride and financial nerve center—for a few weeks. Churches were full as people were frightened and humbled—for a few weeks. But we quickly grew complacent again.

It brought to mind a sermon I preached in New York City in 1957 at Madison Square Garden. My text was 2 Chronicles 7:14, and I drew similarities between our disobedience and that of the ancient people. I spoke about the underpinnings of a nation that we claimed to be "under God" and expressed fear that if America did not turn back to God, judgment was ahead.

My message also looked back into history. On September 11, 1777 (exactly 180 years before), the Continental Congress voted to spend three hundred thousand dollars to buy copies of the Bible to be distributed throughout the colonies. This was widely accepted, of course. Even the roots of our educational institutions were based on faith in God.

Harvard University was founded in 1636. In John Harvard's bequest to the school, he left several rules and precepts that were to be observed by the college bearing his name. The second rule states:

Let every Student be plainly instructed, and earnestly pressed to consider well, the main end of his life and studies is, to know God and Jesus Christ which is eternal life . . . and therefore to lay Christ in the bottom as the only foundation of all sound knowledge and Learning.

And seeing the Lord only gives wisdom, let everyone seriously set himself by prayer in secret to seek it of him.

Mr. Harvard wanted higher education to be a place where people would come to study the Bible and acknowledge Christ as Lord and

Savior. And he was not alone. Dartmouth College was founded by an ordained clergyman with a desire to establish a school where Indians of New England could be trained in the truth of the Gospel of Christ. Yale and Columbia (King's College) Universities had similar foundations. What happened? People grew complacent and thought they did not need God anymore.

This is the story of the human race. We want God to bless us, and when He does we gladly accept His blessings. When bad things happen, however, we forget His blessings and blame our bad times on Him. This is why the Lord told Solomon that His people must turn from their wicked ways and humble themselves before He would bring healing.

There are those who are rewriting our rich heritage, arguing that our founders never intended for our nation to be "under God." But our prized documents say otherwise.

During that sixteen-week crusade, I recall looking out of my hotel-room window over the great city of New York and marveling at God's hand of protection on our nation. I reflected on the sight of Berlin, sitting among its rubble after World War II a few years before. I remembered London, just after the flames and the bombs had stopped. And I prayed, "O God, I pray this will never happen to America." And then I looked out the window at the masses of people scurrying around, busy with life, unconcerned about what really mattered—people's souls and where they would spend eternity. I wondered how long God would remain patient.

That was 1957.

Before America was attacked by outside forces in 2001, our nation and our churches were already being attacked from within. No wonder; God has been removed from our schools. For the past many years churches have centered much of their preaching and programs on just about everything but God. While we have grand buildings and congregations, many members of those churches have never encountered Jesus Christ. They are being fooled into thinking they merit God's favor because of their busyness and good works. Many serve God with their lips, but their hearts are far from Him (Matthew 15:8).

Our nation grew strong in an era when moral standards were emphasized but has been weakened by our condoning that which we once condemned. Whenever 2 Chronicles is recited, I pray to God that people will dwell on what the Lord is commanding. We must set aside our pride and humble ourselves to God's will. We must pray with repentant hearts in His presence. We must seek His face for direction in all that we do. We must turn from the wickedness of sin that will destroy us. Then, by faith, we must accept His response with gladness.

The Lord had more to say to Israel, and we must heed these warnings as well.

> But if you turn away and forsake My statutes and My commandments which I have set before you, and go and serve other gods, and worship them, then I will uproot them from My land . . . and this house which I have sanctified for My name I will cast out of My sight. . . .
>
> Everyone who passes by it will . . . say, "Why has the Lord done thus . . . ?" Then they will answer, "Because they forsook the Lord God of their fathers . . . therefore He has brought all this calamity on them." (2 Chronicles 7:19–22)

This was the Lord's Word to ancient Israel, and it is His word to us today.

We may look with a suspicious eye at ancient Israel wanting a king in their own image, but we are no different; we live under a three-ruler kingdom: me, myself, and I.

Just as America has grown and prospered within the framework of our constitution, so Christianity has flourished from the principles set forth in the Bible. The secret strength of a godly nation is found in the faith that abides in the hearts and homes of its citizens. Will we humble ourselves and admit we have strayed too far?

We don't know the future for America, but we do know the future for the people of God. In Israel's case, God will do what He said he would do:

protect the remnant of Israel and restore the throne of David. Who are Israel's remnant? True and faithful believers. The Lord promised Israel that if they obeyed Him there would always be a king on the throne in Israel (1 Kings 9:5–7).

We know that a pattern of sin followed and that today there is no king in Israel. Thank God that Israel is regathering in the shadows of eternity. We know that the Lord is going to restore the throne and that Jesus Christ will be enthroned and crowned King forever in His kingdom.

> "Behold, the days are coming," says the LORD,
> "That I will raise to David a Branch of righteousness;
> A King shall reign and prosper,
> And execute judgment and righteousness in the
>   earth." (Jeremiah 23:5)

David's life is a glimpse of the coming King. David was not only a shepherd boy; he was also a prophet and king. He knew that one day his descendant—and Savior—Jesus, born in the City of David, would ascend to the throne in the city of His God: Jerusalem. This is a tremendous vision of glory. It is not a dream or fantasy but the very reality of hope (Acts 2:25–31).

Jesus came as a prophet (Luke 4:24). Jesus is our Good Shepherd (John 10:11). And Jesus will come back as King (Revelation 17:14). The King of glory and the kingdom of God will rule the nations of the world. His kingdom is already being built up in the hearts of those who submit, surrender, and serve the King of kings in the kingdom of the ages, and we will worship Him on His everlasting throne.

> Blessed be the LORD God of Israel
> From everlasting to everlasting! (Psalm 41:13)

CHAPTER 8

MERCY ENDURES FOREVER

Retaliate or Rebuild

EZRA, NEHEMIAH, ESTHER

For His mercy endures **forever.**

—EZRA 3:11

Stand up and bless the LORD your God
Forever and ever! *. . .*
For You are God, gracious and merciful.

—NEHEMIAH 9:5, 31

Esther [begged] for mercy and [pleaded] for her people.

—ESTHER 4:8 NLT

THE NEWS CAME AS A TERRIBLE SHOCK. "The wall of Jerusalem is . . . broken down, and its gates are burned with fire" (Nehemiah 1:3). That was the report that came to Nehemiah in the land of Persia. He was devastated.

Just who is this Nehemiah? Probably the most famous captive of his day, who had become a loyal servant in the royal Persian palace. His story is told in one of the most dramatic books of the Old Testament. Nehemiah had been captured in Jerusalem and exiled to a foreign land, then had risen to a highly exalted position to serve the king of Persia as his cupbearer. It meant that the king himself put complete confidence in him.

Nehemiah was loyal, honest, and trustworthy. But despite his great success, he never felt at home in this foreign palace. His heart was in Jerusalem; he belonged to God. So when he received this jolting report that the Jewish city was in great affliction and suffering reproach, Nehemiah knew he had to find a way back home.

So what did he do? He prayed.

"O great and awesome God," he began, "You who keep Your covenant and mercy with those who love You and observe Your commandments. . . . Both my father's house and I have sinned. We have acted very corruptly against You" (vv. 5–7).

It is humbling to read the biblical prayers offered by God's servants, for when they prayed, they assumed responsibility for the people's sins, placing themselves as one with the people. So Nehemiah rehearsed Israel's cycle of sin and remembered God's faithful mercy to them.

"If you are unfaithful," God had told His people, "I will scatter you among the nations; but if you return to Me, and keep My commandments and do them . . . I will gather them from there, and bring them to the place which I have chosen as a dwelling for My name" (vv. 8–9).

That is exactly what had happened. The people of Israel had disobeyed God repeatedly and now were scattered. But a remnant remained in Jerusalem.

Before Nehemiah asked for the king's favor to grant his request to go home, he put his heart's desire before the merciful God who answers prayers. Nehemiah praised the God of Heaven and thanked Him for His faithfulness. He repented of sin—his own and his nation's. He remembered the Lord's judgment for unfaithfulness. He also remembered God's mercy when sinners repent.

The Persian king, out of admiration for Nehemiah, granted his bold request to return to Jerusalem and rebuild the city wall. Nehemiah mounted up and headed home.

Here is an important lesson when we find ourselves among unbelievers, whether in school, at work, or even in the home: we must be a light for God's truth. We must pray that God will grant us favor with those who are watching our lives; that we will stand for the things of God without compromise, and perhaps the Lord will give us opportunities to demonstrate His power, love, and mercy. This is what took place with Nehemiah. And because of his faithfulness, he was called on to speak for the Lord.

Upon his arrival in Jerusalem, Nehemiah found great discouragement among the people because of the opposition from Sanballat, the governor of Samaria, and Tobiah the Ammonite. These two men had given the impression they were for the Jews when in fact they were their enemies. They were grieved when they discovered that Nehemiah had come to help the children of Israel. But nothing deterred Nehemiah, not even their mocking at the ridiculous notion that he could mobilize the people to perform such a monumental task of rebuilding the walls of Jerusalem.

As the wall began to go up, enemy opposition also escalated. Sanballat and Tobiah tried to discourage, distract, and deceive the people. Nehemiah was ridiculed, laughed at, and despised. He knew that Sanballat was trying to destroy the morale of the workers. He not only had to rebuild the physical walls of the city, but a wall of courage had to be raised in the souls of the people. So Nehemiah prayed again, and the Lord gave the people "a mind to work" (4:6).

When ridicule failed to discourage the Israelites, the conspirators changed their tactics and assembled an armed force outside of Jerusalem, taunting and threatening the workers. But Nehemiah recognized their evil ways and set a watch against them day and night. When their intimidation was not successful, they tried to lure Nehemiah out on the plain under the pretense of a conference, saying in essence, "Come down for a meeting of the minds." But again, Nehemiah was watching. He refused their invitation, knowing their evil intent to distract him. He said, "I am doing a great work, so that I cannot come down. Why should the work cease while I leave it and go down to you?" (6:3).

What a tremendous picture this is. The prophet put the priority on God's work, refusing to be tricked into distraction. His work was God's work, so he refused to "go down."

Sanballat was angry to the point of sending a slanderous letter to Nehemiah and revealing the message to everyone, accusing Nehemiah of planning to rebel against the king and become king himself. He taunted Nehemiah with a threat, saying that the king would hear of Nehemiah's evil plan and retaliate.

Again, Nehemiah refused to be provoked. There was no time for retaliation; he was busy building. So he sent back a curt denial of the charges and pressed on with the work, praying that God would strengthen his hands.

Sanballat's next tactic was to bribe other prophets in Jerusalem to deceive Nehemiah and draw him away from the temple so they could attack him. Nehemiah answered, "Should such a man as I flee?" (v. 11). The Lord had given Nehemiah wisdom to see through the devious plot, and he gave thanks to the Lord that he had not been provoked to sin.

Because of Nehemiah's faithfulness, the Lord blessed the people's work, and the wall stood completed in the incredibly short space of fifty-two days. When Nehemiah's enemies heard the news of this success, "they were much cast down . . . for they perceived that this work was wrought of . . . God" (v. 16 KJV).

Now there is much more to Nehemiah's story, but there are three things that often get missed in this account. One is the mercifulness of

God: "He delights in mercy" (Micah 7:18). Nehemiah recognized that it was by the grace and mercy of the Lord that God accomplished great victories. Nehemiah was overwhelmed by the graciousness of the Lord, that he would be used in accomplishing God's great plan. He praised almighty God for His wonderful mercies.

Second, Nehemiah warned the people, "Do not be afraid of [the enemy]. Remember the Lord" (Nehemiah 4:14). He stationed armed guards on the wall, and the workers labored with one hand while they held a weapon in the other. The men were "always on guard" (v. 21 NLT).

This is important to note because the New Testament tells us, "Be sober, be vigilant; because your adversary the devil walks about like a roaring lion, seeking whom he may devour. Resist him, steadfast in the faith" (1 Peter 5:8–9). The Old Testament says, "Sin is crouching at the door, eager to control you. But you must subdue it" (Genesis 4:7 NLT).

You may say, "Well, I have never seen the devil crouching at my door." Are you sure about that? You may not know he is there because you refuse to recognize his clever strategies. Instead of watching for the devil's tactics, you are considering his temptations. What is crouching between the pages of your magazines? What is crouching inside your computer? What is crouching inside the most secret corners of your heart?

Nehemiah's enemies were crouching outside the walls of Jerusalem, and he knew they were there. How? He stayed alert; he was watching from the city walls as the work continued. He and the people had prepared themselves. They had suited up for the battle and did not cave in to the enemy's trickery.

Third, Nehemiah did not fall for the enemy's threats. He refused to be distracted by their insincere overtures to have "a meeting of the minds." He knew their motive was not God honoring. They wanted to prevent the wall and the city from being rebuilt. He also knew their letter to the king was a lie. "There is no truth in any part of your story," he told them. "You are making up the whole thing." According to his own account, "They were just trying to intimidate us, imagining that they could discourage us and stop the work. So I continued the work with even greater determination" (Nehemiah 6:8–9 NLT).

Nehemiah had confidence in what the Lord had asked him to do, and he would not allow the enemy to get him off track. This strengthened the people of Jerusalem, and a marvelous victory was achieved. When the wall was finished, they assembled "with a unified purpose" and "asked Ezra the scribe to bring out the Book of the Law of Moses" that Israel was to obey (8:1 NLT). Ezra mounted a high platform that had been built for the occasion. And when he opened the Word of God, all the men, women, and children worshiped the Lord as Ezra read from the book, and they wept.

Many hours later, the leaders said to the people,

> Stand up and bless the LORD your God,
> Forever and ever! (9:5)

And then they prayed, recalling all that God had done for Israel:

> You are a God of forgiveness, gracious and merciful, slow to become angry, and rich in unfailing love. . . .
> In your great mercy, you sent them liberators who rescued them from their enemies. . . .
> In your wonderful mercy, you rescued them many times! . . .
> In your great mercy, you did not destroy them completely or abandon them forever. What a gracious and merciful God you are! (vv. 17–31 NLT)

What a wonderful trio: mercy, mercy, and mercy.

We see the ever-present mercies of God demonstrated, even in the days of Queen Esther. Her uncle, Mordecai, had refused to bow to the wickedness of a man in authority over him (Esther 3:2). He and Esther both were willing to put their lives in jeopardy to protect their people. The Lord raised Mordecai up to a place of honor in the kingdom (9:4), just as He had done with Nehemiah and, centuries earlier, with Joseph—for the purpose of keeping His eternal promise to Israel.

God places His people strategically—even in pagan societies—giving them opportunities to be obedient and stand up for the glory of His name. God's Word proves faithful, true, and forever merciful.

His mercy is on those who fear Him
From generation to generation. (Luke 1:50)

CHAPTER 9

ETERNAL REDEMPTION

Sackcloth, Ashes, and Joy

JOB

Oh, that my words were written!
. . . inscribed in a book!
*. . . **forever!***
For I know that my Redeemer lives.

—JOB 19:23–25

I WISH I HAD PREACHED MORE ON THE RESURRECTION OF CHRIST BECAUSE WITHOUT IT, THERE WOULD BE NO GOSPEL. It is the resurrection that completes the work that Jesus came to do so that we can live a resurrected life now. Christ did not stay on the cross. He was raised from the dead; He is alive!

In his last year as chancellor of Germany, Konrad Adenauer invited me for a visit. It surprised me that he knew I existed. When we met, he looked at me with his blazing eyes and said, "Young man, I've invited you for one thing. I want to know, do you believe in the resurrection of Jesus Christ?"

I said, "I do, sir!"

He replied, "So do I!" Then he made a powerful declaration: "Life has no meaning whatsoever if Christ is still in the grave!"

The risen Savior has promised to give immortality to all who believe on His name. No longer do people need to stumble in the fog of hopelessness. There is a light that shines brighter than the noonday sun, and Christ's resurrection is what gives us hope; this is the first stage of eternal life in Him. The first glorious step on the journey is choosing Christ. "For if we have been united together in the likeness of His death, certainly we also shall be in the likeness of His resurrection" (Romans 6:5).

Here is an age-old question, found in the Old Testament book of Job: "If a man dies, shall he live again?" (14:14). We expect death, but we usually have a glimmer of hope that medical science will discover something that will keep us alive a little longer. Death carries with it a certain dread. From the day that Cain killed Abel, people have dreaded death. Death brings great fear to many. It can be a mysterious monster that haunts the living.

Many Bible passages bring comfort at the time of death, but the Bible also links sin with death. Paul wrote, "The sting of death is sin" (1 Corinthians 15:56) and "Through one man sin entered the world . . . thus death spread to all men, because all sinned" (Romans 5:12).

Death stalks the rich and the poor, the educated and the uneducated. It is no respecter of race, color, or creed. Its shadow lurks day and night. We never know when the moment of death will come for us.

How do we know there is something more beyond death? Look into the garden tomb, outside of that great walled city. Jesus had been buried there, and a few women came that first Easter to anoint the Lord's body. They were startled to find the tomb empty. An angel sat on the stone that had been rolled away from the door of the tomb and said, "I know that you seek Jesus who was crucified. He is not here; for He is risen, as He said" (Matthew 28:5–6).

The greatest news that mortal ears have ever heard is that Jesus Christ has risen from the dead. Only in this truth can we comprehend that out of death comes life, out of emptiness comes eternity.

Had the tomb not been empty, the promise would have been broken, unfulfilled, leaving no one with hope. The fulfillment of the promise that Christ would be resurrected is the very foundation of the Gospel. Doctrines of the Christian faith are vital, but the resurrection is essential. Without an ironclad belief in Christ's victory over the grave, there can be no personal salvation. Hearts are filled with joy unspeakable because of the empty tomb.

This is where the answer to Job's question is found—that because Christ lives, we also shall live. Job testified in faith to this future reality:

> Oh, that my words were written!
> Oh, that they were inscribed in a book!
> That they were engraved on a rock
> With an iron pen and lead, forever!
> For I know that my Redeemer lives,
> And He shall stand at last on the earth . . .
> That in my flesh I shall see God . . .
> And my eyes shall behold. . . .
> How my heart yearns within me! (Job 19:23–27)

Can't you just feel the pulsating thrill in Job's expression? Centuries before Jesus died and rose again, bringing mankind newness of life, Job believed the promise. Job wanted his witness of the resurrection, through faith in God's promises, to live forever. And now, thousands of years later, we are still reading Job's words engraved on the Rock, Christ Jesus.

Though Job had experienced every catastrophe life could bring—death of his entire family; loss of his home, business, and wealth; illness; accusations from friends; and attacks on his faith in God—still he said,

> Though He slay me, yet will I trust Him. . . .
> He also shall be my salvation. (13:15–16)

Job may have been dressed in sackcloth and sitting among the ashes, but his mind was on the joy of eternity.

We cannot avoid suffering, but we can determine our response to it. We can react with bitterness and hate God, as some do, or we can accept suffering as a natural part of life and know that God can use it for good. We can experience the joy of this truth when we realize that He gives us the power to trust Him.

No matter the mess we may make of our lives, Christ's redemption leaves our transgressions against Him trampled in the dirt and dust, and eternity emerges. Our faces become the faces in which the resurrected Christ shows forth His beauty and His glory.

In my years of global travels, I have seen a world in pain. Without God's guidance, our response to suffering is a futile attempt to find solutions to conditions that cannot be solved. When suffering comes to us, we need to entrust each day to God with prayer and praise on our lips.

Job suffered more than most. There was not one glimmer of hope given to him from those around him. But while he suffered depression and physical pain, he remembered, "My Redeemer lives!" God listened to his pleas and answered his questions—and his prayers.

Why? First, Job's eyes were on the Lord.

> I have made a covenant with my eyes. . . .
> For what is . . . the inheritance of the Almighty from
>   on high? (31:1–2)

Our eyes become the eyes of the resurrected Christ, to exhibit His sympathy and His tenderness. Your eyes should never be lent to the devil; they belong to God. Be careful how you use your eyes.

Second, Job committed the words of his lips to the Lord. "'Shall we indeed accept good from God, and shall we not accept adversity?' In all this Job did not sin with his lips" (2:10). Our lips become the lips of the resurrected Christ, to speak His messages; harsh, unkind words should remain unspoken. Our speech should reflect Christ, giving testimony that causes others to marvel at the gracious words that come out of our mouths.

When Jesus was on earth, the people said, "No man ever spoke like this Man!" (John 7:46). This is the One who lives within believers. His words are spirit and life. Your lips, too, are His; they should never be lent to the devil.

Third, Job tuned his ears to the living Lord:

> I have heard of You by the hearing of the ear,
> But now my eye sees You. (Job 42:5)

Our ears become the ears of the resurrected Christ. They will be sensitive to every cry of spiritual need. Take heed what you hear. Refuse to hear the voice of the tempter. Your ears are His as well; never lend them to the devil.

Fourth, Job focused his mind on the Source of all wisdom:

> Who has put wisdom in the mind?
> Or who has given understanding to the heart? (38:36)

Our minds become the mind of the resurrected Christ. The Bible says, "Let this mind be in you which was also in Christ Jesus" (Philippians 2:5).

Cultivate spiritual thinking. Your intellect becomes His so that you may be an instrument for His purposes. Yield your mind to Him so that you may know His secrets and be kept in His will. Never lend your mind to the devil; the mind is the devil's favorite avenue of attack. Keeping your mind focused on God is essential to protecting your spirit.

> You have granted me life and favor,
> And Your care has preserved my spirit. (Job 10:12)

Finally, Job recognized the importance of putting his hands to God's purposes:

> The righteous will hold to his way,
> And he who has clean hands will be stronger and
>   stronger. (17:9)

Our hands become the hands of the resurrected Christ, to act on His impulse. He will work through us. The apostle Paul said that the same power that raised Christ from the dead is ours, enabling us to live for Him.

We must allow Christ to allocate our time as His own; to control our money as His own; to energize our talents, our zeal, and our ability with His resurrected life; to have complete right-of-way throughout our being. He does not want an apartment in our house; He claims our entire home from attic to cellar. Almighty God reserves the right to wholly give and take away.

Job was a man who had firsthand experience with the God of hope, his resurrected Redeemer, which led him to proclaim, "Behold, happy is the man whom God corrects" (5:17).

Before eternity fully embraces us on the other side of this life, we can experience a resurrected life because Christ lives in all believers who follow Him. Call upon His resources. His grace is more than sufficient. Through disappointments and trials, through all the circumstances of life, Christ will go with you if you will put your trust in Him by faith. He will cause you always to triumph over the world, the flesh, and the devil. Let Him transform your life so that you will have a glow on your face, a spring in your step, and joy in your soul.

God restored Job and gave him greater possessions than he had at the first. But even before that happened, Job told the Lord,

> I know that You can do everything,
> And that no purpose of Yours can be withheld from
>   You. (42:2)

Suffering in life can uncover untold depths of character and unknown strength for service. People who go through life unscathed by sorrow and untouched by pain tend to be shallow in their perspectives on life. Suffering, on the other hand, tends to plow up the surfaces of people's lives and uncover the depths that provide greater strength of purpose and accomplishment. Only deeply plowed earth can yield a bountiful harvest.

No one—not even Job—has ever suffered as much as Jesus. No one has ever loved as deeply as Christ. No one can redeem souls bound for Hell except the Savior. He resurrects souls steeped in sin, and His resurrection work empowers us today and will be never ending.

You, O LORD, are our Father;
Our Redeemer from Everlasting is Your name. (Isaiah 63:16)

CHAPTER 10

JOY ETERNAL

Preparing for Home

In Your presence is fullness of joy;
At Your right hand are pleasures **forevermore**.

—PSALM 16:11

THOSE WHO KEEP HEAVEN IN VIEW EXPERIENCE JOY, EVEN IN THE MIDST OF TROUBLE. Happiness can be fleeting, but joy runs deep; it is one of the fruits of the Spirit. The ability to rejoice in any situation is a sign of spiritual maturity.

This was never more evident than with my friend Billie Barrows, especially in the months leading up to her death. Cliff and Billie Barrows joined me in ministry while on their honeymoon in 1945. It was the beginning of a long and joyful friendship. Cliff directed our music, and Billie played the piano in those early days. Their ministry among the team was marked by joy—how appropriate, since joy often accompanies music. The Old Testament is filled with music, and King David was, perhaps, the very first music director, who appointed singers "by raising the voice with resounding joy" (1 Chronicles 15:16).

My goodness, what a wonderful description of Cliff Barrows! He certainly has known how to mobilize enormous choirs and motivate them to lift their voices in thunderous joy. I miss that marvelous and heavenly music.

After forty-nine years of marriage and service together with our team, Billie Barrows transcended this life into eternity. Following the glorious music at the 1994 memorial service that celebrated her life, I was asked to make some remarks.

She had departed from the land of the dying. This is true for the Christian. I cannot help but think of the powerful words widely attributed to John Newton as he lay on his deathbed. Someone asked him, "Are you still with us?" Newton whispered, "I am still in the land of the dying, but soon, I shall be in the land of the living!"

You see, death for the Christian is just the entryway to eternity, where the eternal God in the heavens welcomes us in. The Bible says, "He who hears My word and believes in Him who sent Me has everlasting life, and shall not come into judgment, but has passed from death into life" (John 5:24).

Ruth and I visited the Barrows in their home shortly before Billie's death. They were expecting their children home for a few days of reunion. Billie knew she did not have long on this earth.

I stayed downstairs with Cliff as he fixed lunch, while Ruth went upstairs with Billie, who had been preparing some of the children's rooms. She was so happy and filled with joy as she anticipated her children's visit.

How much more does our heavenly Father anticipate His children's homecoming? What joy He must have in preparing our place in Heaven. This is why our mourning is turned to comfort. We who are left behind call death a "homegoing," but the Lord has prepared a marvelous "homecoming." Our imaginations simply cannot be stretched enough to comprehend the grandeur of this wonderful home, but in our limited language it means we will go on forever, in a place of everlasting joy, contentment, and peace.

We are given this hope and assurance in 1 Corinthians 2:9:

> Eye has not seen, nor ear heard,
> Nor have entered into the heart of man
> The things which God has prepared for those who love
>   Him.

The apostle Paul could clearly speak to this because he had been "caught up to the third heaven." He said that Heaven was so glorious that he could not describe it (2 Corinthians 12:2–4). Paul was reluctant to speak of his experience; but under the instruction of the Holy Spirit he wrote,

> [I] heard things so astounding that they cannot be expressed in words, things no human is allowed to tell.
>
> That experience is worth boasting about, but I'm not going to do it. . . . I don't want anyone to give me credit beyond what they can see in my life or hear in my message, even though I have received such wonderful revelations from God. (vv. 4–7 NLT)

This should be a lesson for us when we are tempted to applaud accounts of those who claim to have gone to Heaven and returned to tell about it in detail. God's Word has pulled the curtain back just enough to show us a glimpse of that heavenly land.

No more curses, no more sin, no more death, no more pain, no more sorrow, and no more loneliness. The gates will be eternally open; they will not be shut at all by day, for there will be no night there (Revelation 21:25)—in other words, no night of sin, no night of sorrow, no night of death. This is Heaven eternal.

We will know morning glories that never cease because the Son will shine His eternal light upon us forever, and all of Heaven will be filled with resounding joy. Being in His presence will be our treasure. I look forward to that.

But while we remain earthbound, believers are the most privileged to spread His message of mercy and forgiveness, hope and joy, knowing that when one sinner repents, there is joy in Heaven (Luke 15:7). How can we ever begin to know the rejoicing that will take place when the Lord brings all of us home in immortal bodies? The morning stars will sing together and the angels will shout for glory. The Bible says,

> In Your presence is fullness of joy;
> At Your right hand are pleasures forevermore.
> (Psalm 16:11)

Think of having complete fulfillment, knowing that our homecoming brings unspeakable joy to our wonderful Lord! Only when we stand in the joyful presence of Jesus Christ will this be realized. So why do we prefer lingering here? Because we are not only earthbound in body; we are earthbound in our thinking. Our imagination is limited to the things of this earth. But when we leave this place, we will never dwell on it again. Our eyes and hearts will be fixed on Christ.

Someone wrote when his spouse died, "Should you go first and I remain, walk slowly down that path, for soon I will follow you." I thought about that when my wife, Ruth, died in 2007. I never thought I would live so many years without her. But I know Ruth would never have walked slowly, waiting for me to catch up. She would be too anxious to see Christ. She knows that when I follow, I will find her before the throne of God.

Before Jesus raised his friend Lazarus from the dead, He told Martha, "Your brother will rise again" (John 11:23). He was telling her about an even greater miracle to come, when all the dead in Christ will be called out of their graves. This is the believer's great hope. Christians who die physically go on living joyfully, forever in Christ's presence. Because of Him we have hope beyond tears, hope beyond sorrow, and hope beyond today.

I am reminded of a hymn that has brought so much comfort:

Beyond the sunset, O glad reunion
With our dear loved ones who've gone before;
In that fair homeland we'll know no parting—
Beyond the sunset forevermore!¹

This was the thought that brought comfort to Billie Barrows, and she asked that it be read at her service:

As for me, I will see Your face in righteousness;
I shall be satisfied when I awake in Your likeness.
　(Psalm 17:15)

When that time comes for you, will you rejoice to see Christ face-to-face? Or will you remember the moment when you denied Him and refused to accept the hope of eternal life with Him? Receive Him with joy today.

When we stand at the graveside of a loved one, we sorrow. But those united with Christ in death are also united with Him in the joy of resurrection. There was no joy at the tomb of Lazarus. It was a somber and woeful time—until Jesus arrived! Mary and Martha had wept for their loss, and Jesus had delayed His appearance for the purpose of demonstrating His power over death and sorrow. He said to His disciples, "Our friend Lazarus sleeps, but I go that I may wake him up" (John 11:11).

When Jesus arrived, He comforted Martha with His words:

"I am the resurrection and the life. He who believes in Me, though he may die, he shall live. And whoever lives and believes in Me shall never die. Do you believe this?"

　She said to Him, "Yes, Lord, I believe that You are the Christ, the Son of God." (vv. 25–27)

Then the Lord cried out, "Lazarus, come forth!" (v. 43).
Words cannot describe the shock of seeing a dead man alive again—

and the joy of knowing that we, too, shall one day hear the Lord Jesus call our names. Contemplate it for a moment and imagine hearing His voice speak your name. If that does not cause joy to bubble inside of you, it is doubtful anything else will.

There is a solemn but glorious scene in the book of Acts. As Stephen was being stoned for his witness of Christ, he cried out to the Lord to forgive his persecutors. He looked into Heaven and saw Jesus standing there (Acts 7:56). What a vision that must have been. The Lord Jesus Christ stood to welcome Stephen, the first martyr, into His kingdom. That is joy—eternal joy!

So I would ask you: Are you preparing for home? If so, then you will say:

Therefore my heart is glad, and my glory rejoices;
My flesh also will rest in hope. (Psalm 16:9)

CHAPTER 11

WISDOM ETERNAL IN HEAVEN

I Am Wisdom

PROVERBS

I have been established from **everlasting** *...*
before there was ever an earth. . . .
When He prepared the heavens, I was there.

—PROVERBS 8:23, 27

HEAVEN CAPTURES THE IMAGINATION, BUT IT IS NOT AN IMAGINARY PLACE. It is not a fantasyland in which to dwell. It is not a place one can travel to and come back again—at least not in our earthbound life. Heaven is a literal place.

The eighth chapter of Proverbs is deep and wide because it is the voice of wisdom speaking to our hearts. It is the Lord Jesus Himself gathering up His eternal attributes that call out to us with His understanding, truth, righteousness, knowledge and instruction, prudence and discretion, reverence, counsel, strength, love, riches and honor, justice, rejoicing, blessing, wisdom, and eternal life. This is what Heaven is and will be forever:

> Does not wisdom cry out? (v. 1)
> My voice is to the sons of men. (v. 4)
> For I will speak of excellent things. (v. 6)
> Those who seek me diligently will find me. (v. 17)
> When He prepared the heavens, I was there. (v. 27)
> When . . . the waters would not transgress His command,
> When He marked out the foundations of the earth,
> Then I was beside Him as a master craftsman.
>   (vv. 29–30)
> Blessed is the man who listens to me. (v. 34)

We see these wonderful claims in John 1:3–4: "All things were made through Him, and without Him nothing was made that was made. In Him was life."

Bible writers wrote of this eternal place where wisdom both dwells and calls out to mankind. Wisdom can also enter our hearts (Proverbs 2:10), and that is why those who possess the Lord Jesus Christ will be very much at home in God's Heaven.

Abraham did not cling to the promise of living in a state of mind. He looked forward to "the city which has foundations, whose architect and builder is God" (Hebrews 11:10 NASB). The Old Testament heroes of faith longed for a better place in a better land—Heaven.

But regardless of the pictures that come to mind, we cannot fathom this glorious place. Not even the greatest artist's rendering can capture its grandeur. What we are incapable of comprehending, God holds in His hands. "Behold, heaven and the heaven of heavens cannot contain You" (1 Kings 8:27). All of creation is dwarfed in His presence.

Generations have been thrilled with the song, "He's got the whole world in His hands." Yes, the whole world takes up just a smidgen.

Who has measured the waters in the hollow of His hand,

Measured heaven with a span? . . .

The nations are as a drop in a bucket. (Isaiah 40:12, 15)

The Bible tells us that God set "a firmament in the midst of the waters," divided "the waters from the waters," and "called the firmament Heaven" (Genesis 1:6–8). The word *firmament* is one we are not accustomed to hearing anymore; it comes from the Hebrew word meaning firm or fixed.

More important than Heaven capturing our imagination is the God of Heaven capturing our souls. Just because Heaven is beyond the reach of our satellites and telescopes does not mean that Heaven is beyond the reach of our hearts. The key to finding Heaven is finding Christ.

Today's technology has surpassed me. I am amazed to get into an automobile and see a moving map on the dashboard. Macular degeneration prevents my eyes from following the details, and my ears cannot distinctly hear the voice commands, but I know it works. This device informs the driver how long the trip will take, instructs when to turn, and even announces the arrival.

My friend, there is a heavenly GPS that will bring you safely to your eternal destination in Heaven. It is called the Gospel Plan of Salvation. It only has one direction—up—and the Navigator, the Lord Jesus Christ, is "the way" (John 14:6). He appoints the time of arrival and has prepared all that is necessary to welcome us.

By nature, people are bent toward home. When we finish our day and evening activities, we generally head for our homes. Far better than any dream you can imagine is the supernatural transformation that will take place for all of God's people when He transports us to His heavenly home.

We are assured that in Heaven we will be living in God's dwelling place forever, and it will be glorious beyond description. It will be greater than any earthly palace or mansion.

Kings are confined to living in palaces. Owners of vast properties live on estates behind locked gates. God's Word, however, says that Christ will make us joint heirs in the kingdom of God (Romans 8:17). And just as God's habitation extends beyond the boundaries of creation, so will ours—without confinement.

He is the Landowner of Heaven, earth, and the whole universe; and He is going to share all of it with His people. No earthly court, no Wall Street investor, no astute accountant could ever calculate the extent of God's estate, for it is priceless and without limit.

Jesus told His disciples, "And I bestow upon you a kingdom, just as My Father bestowed one upon Me, that you may eat and drink at My table in My kingdom" (Luke 22:29–30). John wrote about the wonderful aspects of Heaven in the book of Revelation. Yes, there is much mystery and untold wonder and glory. But what I do not want you to miss is the door to Heaven. It is open for you. The Bible says, "Behold, a door standing open in heaven" (Revelation 4:1). My friend, that door is the Lord Jesus Christ. If you do not open the door to your heart here on earth, you will never be able to walk through the door that is standing open in Heaven.

Do not miss spending eternity in the "house of the LORD" (Psalm 23:6). The day we step through the gates of splendor, we will be free of the confinements of earth. That's Wisdom eternal—in Heaven!

The angel . . . raised up his hand to heaven and
swore by Him who lives forever and ever,
who created heaven and the things that are in it . . .
that there should be delay no longer. (Revelation 10:5–6)

CHAPTER 12

ETERNITY SET IN THE HEART

Stealing or Sealing the Heart

ECCLESIASTES, SONG OF SOLOMON

*He has also set **eternity** in their heart.*

—ECCLESIASTES 3:11 NASB

Set me as a seal upon your heart.

—SONG OF SOLOMON 8:6

SOMEDAY A LOVING HAND WILL BE LAID UPON YOUR SHOULDER, AND THIS BRIEF MESSAGE WILL BE GIVEN: "COME HOME."

Jesus made a declaration to His disciples about the great mystery of death. After more than two thousand years, His words strike a harmonious chord in human hearts that bring eternal hope and anticipation.

I have preached from chapter 14 of the book of John many times at funeral and memorial services. It is in this great book that Jesus was preparing the disciples for His death, but they didn't grasp it until He had gone away.

Jesus had been heralded as He entered the holy city of Jerusalem on the day we now call Palm Sunday. His disciples were enthralled with the enthusiastic reception the Lord received. They began talking among themselves about who might be the greatest, to sit on either side of the Lord in His coming kingdom. With each passing day as events led to Jesus' crucifixion, He spoke of His coming death. But the twelve were too pre-occupied with their own expectations to comprehend the suffering Jesus was about to face. When He kept telling them that He was going away, the disciples were perplexed. He had just been hailed as the Messiah. Why would He be going away? They were overcome with uncertainty, but He set aside His own anguish and comforted their souls.

Jesus came to earth for the purpose of preparing hearts for eternity. Shortly before He laid down His own life that we might have life, He said, "Let not your heart be troubled. . . . I go to prepare a place for you" (John 14:1–2).

I gave remarks at the memorial service of First Lady Pat Nixon, and these words brought comfort to President Richard Nixon and his two lovely daughters, Tricia and Julie, as they said their earthly good-byes to this dedicated wife and loving mother.[1]

I had known Pat Nixon since the early 1950s. It was hard to imagine this family without her. It seemed surreal to stand before them in June 1993. I had no idea at the time that I would return ten months later to speak at her husband's funeral at the Richard Nixon Library in Yorba Linda, California.

When we are confronted with the death of someone we love, we all pause at least briefly to consider eternity. In these moments Jesus speaks words of comfort to our grieving hearts. Children especially long to hear words of comfort when parents go away. That's why they ask, "Where are you going? Can I go with you? Who is going to stay with me?"

Jesus realized this. In the Upper Room, the evening before He gave

Himself up to die on the cross, He had a meal with His disciples, whom He called "children." (In death's presence, we are all children with uncertainties.) Jesus spoke of His soon departure and promised them, "The Father . . . will give you another Helper, that He may abide with you forever" (v. 16).

Jesus knew that these men would have difficulty coping with His death. He Himself had wept at the graveside of Lazarus, but His tears were not for the dead but for those grieving.

Death will come to us all. That is why we need the hope that Jesus gives. When death comes knocking, do we know where we will go? Jesus gives us this certainty if we belong to Him. Hope in death means that the Lord will turn our pain to joy. When we enter His house, there will be plenty of room, and He tells us we can abide with Him.

Solomon said long ago that the day of a man's death is greater than the day of his birth (Ecclesiastes 7:1), and he penned these words of comfort: "[God] has made everything beautiful in its time. . . . He has [set] eternity in their hearts" (3:11). Nothing brings more consolation to our saddened hearts than to imagine the glory of being in the eternal presence of God.

While the passing of Mrs. Nixon was sorrowful, she had peace in her heart and a sense of eternity beyond. Her passing drew attention to the strong values she demonstrated in her own way. Such moments give us permission to pause and consider what a person's life has meant.

Mike Wallace of CBS once told me that of all the people he had met, he admired Pat Nixon the most. *Time* magazine once profiled her in a cover story and stated that "her stamina and courage, her drive and control have made her one of [America's] most remarkable women."[2]

As I spoke that day, I said, "In your memoirs, Mr. President, you wrote that the Secret Service's code name for her was Starlight. What a fitting description for a delightful lady."

Some years ago Ruth and I were guests of the Nixons at their apartment on Fifth Avenue in New York, and we all had been invited to the home of Jack and Miriam Parr to watch the opening show of Jack's new series. Ruth and I returned with the Nixons afterward to their apartment, where they later put us on an elevator that would take us to our hotel room—but the elevator got stuck halfway between two floors.

We punched all the buttons, hollered, kicked the sides of the elevator, pounded, and yelled for help. I can tell you we needed rescue. After twenty minutes or so, the Nixons showed up in their bathrobes and immediately took over. Pat was the one who seemed to know what to do as she helped us get the elevator down. She was a resourceful woman who knew how to handle herself in a crisis.

At her funeral, as I reminisced about the amazing woman she was, I was reminded of the words of King Solomon, "The memory of the just is blessed" (Proverbs 10:7 KJV). Few women in public life had suffered as she had with such grace. In all the years of friendship, I never heard her say anything unkind about anyone.

When Mrs. Nixon and I flew at the President's request to Liberia on Air Force Two to represent him and the United States at the inauguration of the president of Liberia, she spoke eloquently of her love for Dick and her family. The Nixons' longtime friend and housekeeper told the family a few hours after Pat's death that in her native country she had been taught not to express emotions. "It was Mrs. Nixon," she said, "who taught me to say, 'I love you.'"

So in the midst of death, there is loving remembrance. We all leave footprints behind. For the Christian believer who has been to the cross, death is no frightful leap in the dark but entrance into a glorious new life. The apostle Paul recognized the truth of eternity set in his heart when he said, "For to me, to live is Christ, and to die is gain" (Philippians 1:21).

For the believer, the brutal fact of death has been conquered by the resurrection of Jesus Christ. For the person who has turned from sin and has received Christ as Lord and Savior, death is not the end. For the believer there is hope beyond the grave. There is future life!

After Christ rose from the grave, the apostles began expressing the death of believers in the image frame of being "home with the Lord"

(2 Corinthians 5:8 NASB). God would not have placed eternity in our hearts unless there was life beyond the grave.

During World War II, a mother took her son every day into the bedroom, where hung a large portrait of the boy's father. They would stand and gaze at the image of a man who was fighting for freedom. One day the boy looked up and said, "Mama, wouldn't it be great if Dad could just step down out of the frame?"

For centuries mankind has looked into the heavens to see if God would step out of the frame. At Bethlehem, two thousand years ago, He did. He is the only true visitor from outer space—God incarnate. And in His coming, He changed everything we knew about death.

It is dangerous for people to dodge the subject of death. It is the most important thing in life to resolve: Where will death lead me? Eternity has to be decided on earth. Instead, people stay busy day and night to avoid thinking about their eternal destinations. For believers, our destination is "set," and no one can steal our inheritance from us. We know that we are in a temporary place—pilgrims and strangers in a foreign land. This world is not our home. Our citizenship is in Heaven.

The Bible speaks of a believer's death in several ways.

Death is a coronation. The picture here is that of a great prince who, after his struggles and conquest in an alien land, comes to his native country to be crowned and honored for his deeds. His future is set.

Death is a cessation from labor. The Scripture says, "Blessed are the dead who die in the Lord. . . . that they may rest from their labors" (Revelation 14:13). The Lord of the harvest says to weary workers, "You have been faithful in your task. Come and sit in the sheltered porch of my palace and rest from your labors" (Matthew 25:21, author's paraphrase).

Death is a departure from temporary living. The apostle Paul said, "The time of my departure is at hand" (2 Timothy 4:6).

Many times Pat would kiss Dick as he said good-bye to his family to go on another trip or to attend another important meeting. Separation always meant a twinge of sadness for them both, but there was always high hope that they would meet again. Ruth and I experienced the same hope each time we said good-bye.

Death is a transition. Here we are as pilgrims, living in a frail, flimsy house, subject to disease, pain, and peril. But at death we exchange this crumbling, disintegrating tent for a house not made with hands, eternal in the heavens.

Death is an exodus. We speak of "deceased" as though it were the end of everything, but the word *decease* literally means exodus or going out. The imagery is that of the children of Israel thousands of years ago leaving Egypt and its slavery and hardships. They were on the move toward the Promised Land. So death to the Christian is an exodus from the limitations, the perils, and the bondage of this life.

Tricia Nixon Cox said of her mother, "Her faith in God sustained her during the last difficult years of her life." Julie Nixon Eisenhower wrote, "My mother had a phrase that she used countless times to end conversations with her White House staff members throughout my father's presidency: 'Onward and upward.'"[3]

What a beautiful description of eternity in Heaven. For the Christian, death can be faced realistically and with victory because we know that "neither death nor life . . . [can] separate us from the love of God" (Romans 8:38-39).

Make sure that eternity is sealed in your heart.

Surely goodness and mercy shall follow me
All the days of my life;
And I will dwell in the house of the LORD
Forever. (Psalm 23:6)

Soul Eternal

————————————— *The Life of a Spirit* —

Isaiah

Incline your ear, and come to Me.
Hear, and your soul shall live. . . .
Be glad and rejoice **forever** *in what I create.*

—Isaiah 55:3; 65:18

EVERY SOUL HAS A STORY TO TELL. Some are gruesome; others miraculous. I live in the mountains of North Carolina, and it is not unusual to hear of campers and hikers losing their way along trails that wind through the rugged forests, thick with brush and prone to rock slides. It doesn't take long for people to panic, wondering if they will ever be found.

If you found yourself wandering around in the forest with no food or water, no compass, and no communication device, would you be content to remain lost? If someone suddenly called out your name, would you remain hidden? It's doubtful. You would run toward the sound of the voice.

God is calling lost souls to come to Him. Just as He called out to Adam and Eve, He sends out the rescue call to us.

The world is filled with lost and wandering souls. What preparation have you made for your soul? If you stop and listen with your ears and your heart, you will hear God's voice. If you ignore Him, you are gambling with your eternal future. If you have rebelled against God, please do not close this book until you open your heart to Him, because you may not live long enough to go to the Father and be reconciled.

Jesus has His hand outstretched, waiting for the lost to come to Him. When we start down the road to repentance, He does not cast us off and forsake us. He is there to meet us and welcome us home. The Bible says, "If you seek Him, He will be found by you; but if you forsake Him, He will cast you off forever" (1 Chronicles 28:9).

The day is coming when every soul will give account before the throne of God. Our souls are His very creation and are more valuable to Him than anything. Our bodies are flesh and bone; they will die eventually. But we are also spirit—that includes our conscience, as well as the part of us that thinks and feels. At the time of death, the spirit returns to its Maker (Ecclesiastes 12:7).

When God created Adam's body, it was a house without a resident until God breathed life into him and Adam "became a living soul" (Genesis 2:7 KJV). We cannot see or touch the soul physically, but it is the real you, the real me.

Have you ever wanted to go somewhere but were just too tired? Your body stayed home, but your thoughts were where you really wanted to be. This is a picture of the separation of body and soul. The body will be buried in the earth awaiting the final resurrection, but the soul will be in one of two states: in turmoil waiting for the judgment or at rest in God's care.

The Bible references the heart and soul as the very essence of man. Psalm 13:2 (NLT) speaks of the anguish of soul with sorrow in the heart, and the writer of Lamentations longs for the God who "restores my soul" (1:16 NASB). The Bible tells us that the "soul thirsts" (42:2) and the "soul . . . seeks" (Ecclesiastes 7:28). According to Proverbs 16:24, "Kind words are like honey—sweet to the soul" (NLT).

The prophet Isaiah spoke of the soul with eternity in mind. And he sent out God's message to mankind to respond to God's call. It is a wonderful invitation:

> Everyone who thirsts,
> Come to the waters. . . .
> Let your soul delight itself in abundance.
> Incline your ear, and come to Me.
> Hear, and your soul shall live. (Isaiah 55:1–3)

Think of all the time we spend pampering our bodies. Then think about all the times we have neglected our souls. The Bible says, "For what profit is it to a man if he gains the whole world, and loses his own soul? Or what will a man give in exchange for his soul?" (Matthew 16:26).

Ask yourself this question: Do you care more for your child's clothes or for the child? Likewise, the body is the covering; the soul is the true person.

The Bible teaches that whether we are saved or lost, there is consciousness and everlasting existence of the soul and personality. Zechariah wrote, "The LORD . . . forms the spirit of man within him" (12:1). Take care of your soul—your inner self—by feeding on the Word of God and letting His Spirit transform you from within; for the soul has a sixth sense—the ability to believe and to have faith.

The soul, though it cannot be seen or touched, is valuable because it is eternal. Just as the body has many members, so the soul possesses the unseen faculties and attributes: judgment (which makes determinations), the will (which makes choices), affections (which cause us to love or to fear), memory (for storing up knowledge), and the conscience (which monitors and evaluates all we say and think). The Bible describes the soul as "the hidden person of the heart, with the incorruptible beauty of a gentle and quiet spirit, which is very precious in the sight of God" (1 Peter 3:4).

The soul is valuable because of the price paid for its redemption. "For the redemption of [the soul] is costly," wrote the psalmist (49:8). And 2 Peter 3:9 says that God is "not willing that any should perish but that all should come to repentance."

The Scottish preacher John Harper was aboard the *Titanic* in 1912, making his way to preach at Moody Church. When the ship went down, Harper drifted into a young man holding on to a plank.

Harper said, "Young man, are you saved?"

The young man answered, "No."

A wave separated them. After a few minutes they were within speaking distance, and again Harper called out to him: "Has your soul made peace with God?"

The young man said, "Not yet."

A wave overwhelmed John Harper, and he was seen no more. But the words "Are you saved?" kept ringing in the young man's ears. Two weeks later the young man stood up in a youth meeting in New York, told his story, and said, "I am John Harper's last convert."

John Harper knew the value of a soul almost lost at sea. As a result, a young man discovered that the worth of his soul was eternal.

This is why Isaiah wrote,

> Seek the LORD while He may be found,
> Call upon Him while He is near.
> Let the wicked forsake his way,
> And the unrighteous man his thoughts;
> Let him return to the LORD,
> And he will have mercy on him . . .
> For He will abundantly pardon. (55:6–7)

This wonderful invitation was extended not only to the house of Israel but also to all who will turn to God. His kingdom will be filled with souls from every nation, every tribe, and every race. He says,

Even to them I will give in My house
And within My walls a place and a name . . .
I will give them an everlasting name
That shall not be cut off. (Isaiah 56:5)

The soul is valuable because of Satan's interest in it. God has been building His kingdom since the beginning, but the devil is also building his. Even though Satan is a defeated foe, he is still working. This is why Satan disguises himself and the Bible tells us to beware.

Jesus said, "When anyone hears the word of the kingdom, and does not understand it, then the wicked one comes and snatches away what was sown in his heart" (Matthew 13:19). Jesus pictures Satan as an enemy battling and bidding for souls by cleverly appealing to our desires.

Think of what the human race typically chases after—worldly riches and the power they bring. The world's worth is staggering when you consider the wealth of governments, commerce, entertainment, technology, the arts, mineral deposits, treasures of the sea, space exploration, and so forth. There is simply no way to calculate the treasure's sum. And yet one soul is worth more than all of this, and the devil knows it.

Voltaire gained the world of literature, but lost his soul.

Hitler gained a world of power, but lost his soul.

Mao Tse-tung, the Chinese Communist revolutionary, once wrote, "It's not enough to have our people's allegiance; we must possess their very souls." This is what Satan wants—your soul.

Of all the possessions we hold dear, we must hold our souls closest, for they are God's treasure, the only thing we can take out of our earthly experience to Heaven. Your soul is traveling to an eternal destination. Are you paying attention to the signs along the way?

There is a stretch of highway going up into the mountains of western North Carolina that has been under construction for many years. It is rugged terrain. The North Carolina Department of Transportation has the monumental task of blasting through boulders and mangled tree roots to carve a smooth pathway into the high country. Vehicles have been caught in rockslides and temporary road closings. Signs flash through the night, Proceed with Caution, guiding drivers through the winding, twisting maze.

When travelers get to the top of the mountain and see the welcomed sign, End of Construction, they know they are nearing home. I have known many parents in that part of the state who pace the floor, knowing their teenagers are up and down that mountain constantly. Reaching their destinations safely brings relief.

Life, too, can be a bumpy journey. Potholes jolt us. Detours get us off course, and signs warn us of danger ahead. The destination of the soul and spirit is of utmost importance to God, so He offers us daily guidance. Some pay close attention to God's directions; others ignore them and speed past the flashing lights. But everyone eventually arrives at the final destination: death's door, where the soul is separated from the body.

Do we really believe that other people can guide us through treacherous terrain but God cannot? He is there, watching every move we make. The question is, are we aware of Him? He is leading the way, and we are called to "follow His steps" (1 Peter 2:21).

Jesus taught that death is a passage for the spirit into the presence of God (Luke 23:46). The psalmist declared, "God will redeem my soul from the power of the grave" (Psalm 49:15). Are you following the caution signs that God has posted throughout His Guidebook, the Bible? His steps will never lead us astray.

> The highway of the upright is to depart from evil;
> He who keeps his way preserves his soul.
>   (Proverbs 16:17)

Isaiah, too, wrote of such a highway.

> A highway shall be there, and a road,
> And it shall be called the Highway of Holiness.

The unclean shall not pass over it,
But it shall be for others.
Whoever walks the road . . .
Shall not go astray. . . .
The redeemed shall walk there,
And the ransomed of the LORD shall return . . .
With everlasting joy. (35:8–10)

Signposts along life's highway are there for a purpose. When we ignore them, we do so at our own peril. Don't allow Satan to trick you into thinking that the signs are there to prevent you from enjoying life. Not at all. They are posted to keep you from trouble so that you can live life with joy, knowing that someday you will walk the streets of Heaven.

Draw back from Satan, not God. For the Lord has given you a soul—entrust Him with it every step of the way.

"Now the just shall live by faith;
But if anyone draws back,
My soul has no pleasure in him."
But we are not of those who draw back to perdition, but of those
who believe to the saving of the soul. (Hebrews 10:38–39)

CHAPTER 14

EVERLASTING LOVE

Tears That Speak

JEREMIAH, LAMENTATIONS

*I have loved you with an **everlasting** love.*

—JEREMIAH 31:3

His compassions fail not. . . .
*You, O LORD, remain **forever**.*

—LAMENTATIONS 3:22; 5:19

GOD'S LOVE DID NOT BEGIN AT THE CROSS, BUT IN ETERNITY PAST. Before the world was established, before the time clock of civilization began to move, God's love prevailed.

But not until the Good News of Jesus Christ burst onto the human scene was the word *love* understood on earth with such depth, as God coming down to us in human form, an expression of unmerited love.

Our popular music talks constantly about love, yet divorce rates continue to skyrocket. Years ago a pop duo sang a song that insisted they wouldn't live in "A World Without Love." Yet Love came down from Heaven to the whole world, and the world rejected Him.

It was God's love that knew mankind was incapable of obeying His law and loving Him. So in love He promised a Redeemer, a Savior, who would give true love away.

Speak about the love of God and faces light up, but speak of God as a Judge, and attitudes change. There is one thing that God's love cannot do; it cannot forgive the unrepentant sinner. For this reason, God sends things into our lives to block the route to destruction, with holy desire to drive us back to His love.

The seventeenth-century scientist Blaise Pascal said, "If eternal damnation is possible, no sacrifice is too great to prevent that possibility from becoming a reality."[1] That's exactly what the Lord's judgment is about. In the Bible He says,

> With a little wrath I hid My face from you for a
>   moment;
> But with everlasting kindness I will have mercy on
>   you. (Isaiah 54:8)

When we truly love others, we want to please and honor them by the way we act. How we treat people shows whether or not we really care about them. If we truly love Christ, we will want to please and honor Him by the way we live. Even the thought of hurting Him or bringing disgrace to His name will be abhorrent to us.

I am convinced the greatest act of love we can ever demonstrate is to tell others about God's love for them in Christ. When Christ's love fills our hearts, it puts selfishness on the run. "We love Him because He first loved us" (1 John 4:19).

The love of God that reaches man, however, can be entirely rejected. God will not force Himself upon anyone. It is our part to believe; it is our part to receive. Nobody else can do it for us.

There was a woman who cared for an orphan. While waiting to be adopted by this woman, the girl enjoyed beautiful clothes, outings, good food, and security of a lovely home—until her friend taunted her that once she was adopted she would be "stuck" with rules to follow. The rules had been pleasant to her—until then.

When the teenager stood before the judge, she would not agree to abide by the rules required, and she walked away from the woman who had loved her. The woman was crushed as she saw the shadow of a daughter walk away. Distraught over her bad decision, the young girl eventually took her life. The woman who had cared for her had a headstone engraved with the words, "She was almost mine." This is love.

The mystery of God's love would not be a mystery if we knew all the answers. But we do know this: God's love is unchangeable. He knows exactly what we are and loves us anyway. God loves us even if, like that rebellious teenager, we choose to walk away from Him forever—we will not enjoy the luxuries and security of His home.

Unfortunately, many people go through life feeling unloved—and unlovable. Many feel unworthy of love. Sigmund Freud declared, "The communal life of human beings had, therefore, a two-fold foundation: the compulsion to work, which was created by external necessity, and the power of love . . ."[2] "The supreme happiness of life," Victor Hugo said, "consists in the conviction that one is loved."[3] Even if you believe you are not loved, your feelings deceive you. The truth is Jesus loves you—the Bible tells you so: "By this we know love, because He laid down His life for us" (1 John 3:16).

It is a heavy responsibility to proclaim this message of God's everlasting love. I have heard about God's love my entire life, and I have seen it demonstrated. From a young age, my sweet, godly mother taught me my first Bible verse, John 3:16: "For God so loved the world. . . ." Not everyone grows up this way, I know. I have been commissioned to make this message known. Why would I withhold this tremendous Good News?

Some think of love as a warm and touchy—even romantic—emotion.

Others see love through the eyes of an innocent baby completely dependent on its mother. These are outward expressions of love.

Then there are those who define love as stooping down and pulling people out of a dirty ditch and helping them get back on their feet. Sometimes such love is reciprocated, but even if it's not, that doesn't change the fact that the rescuer reached out in compassionate love.

But how about the love demonstrated when an enemy brutally attacks you with words or actions? Does love come easily then? This is the greatest test of love, and this is the love that Christ demonstrated on the cross, to love our enemies.

Then there's the love that dares to deliver a warning, even an unwelcome one. This was the prophet Jeremiah's experience. Jeremiah was chosen by God to proclaim a harsh message, warning God's people of severe consequences unless they changed the way they were living; they must abide with Him and follow His commandments.

Idol worship had led them into sacrificing their own children to the god Molech. For nearly fifty years Jeremiah pronounced God's judgment upon the people if they did not repent. There would be brief times of superficial remorse; then the people reverted back to their iniquity.

God commissioned Jeremiah:

> Whatever I command you, you shall speak.
> Do not be afraid of their faces,
> For I am with you to deliver you. (Jeremiah 1:7–8)

So Jeremiah faithfully preached, "Thus says the LORD. . . . Judah has not turned to Me with her whole heart, but in pretense" (2:5; 3:10).

It was not a popular message, and God's people did not respond well. The Lord knew that their hearts were full of deceit, and they loved it that way. Jeremiah eventually became depressed because of the Lord's longsuffering toward them. It wearied him to watch as they defied God outwardly. He became downtrodden and cursed the day he was born because of the heavy burden placed on him as God's spokesman.

In the poetic book of Lamentations, we sense the anguish of spirit that Jeremiah had in his long ministry among the stiff-necked people who had become enemies of God. Jeremiah became known as the *weeping* prophet. He shed tears that spoke of his anguish of soul. He pleaded with the Lord so that he would not have to speak to the hardened hearts that repeatedly rejected the God who loved "with an everlasting love" (31:3).

God's message indeed was anguishing: "I will pursue them with the sword . . . and I will deliver them to trouble . . . because they have not heeded My words" (29:18–19). And Jeremiah was obliged to repeat it:

> I will certainly bring calamity on this people . . .
> Because they have not heeded My words. (6:19)

> Thus they have loved to wander;
> They have not restrained their feet.
> Therefore the LORD . . . will remember their iniquity now,
> And punish their sins. (14:10)

The sin of the people and Jeremiah's pleas from God went on year after year, decade after decade. Then God told Jeremiah to warn the people yet again, "Behold, I am fashioning a disaster and devising a plan against you. Return now every one from his evil way, and make your ways and your doings good" (18:11).

This is what the Lord does because of His everlasting love. Like a good parent, He punishes the children to protect them from the consequences of further disobedience. "For whom the LORD loves He [disciplines]" (Hebrews 12:6). All His warnings come with pleas to repent and turn to Him. But look at the people's devastating response to the Lord's warnings through Jeremiah: "That is hopeless! So we will walk according to our own plans, and we will every one obey the dictates of his evil heart" (Jeremiah 18:12). The people readily admitted their sin with a vengeful defiance.

Yet even in the midst of this misery we find God's marvelous message to those who would turn to Him:

> Yes, I have loved you with an everlasting love;
> Therefore with lovingkindness I have drawn you. (31:3)

We have all memorized the emergency call number 9-1-1, but we also need to memorize the eternal call number: 33:3. "Call to Me, and I will answer you, and show you great and mighty things, which you do not know" (Jeremiah 33:3). This is a marvelous invitation from our Lord. But He didn't stop there. His invitation was followed by a list of great "I will" promises: I will bring health, I will heal, I will bring abundance of peace and truth, I will rebuild, I will cleanse, I will pardon (vv. 6–8).

Repentance of sin is all it takes to realize God's great love.

King David said,

> The sacrifices of God are a broken spirit,
> A broken and a contrite heart—
> These, O God, You will not despise. (Psalm 51:17)

It is often into broken ground that the seeds of spring are planted; they germinate to grow into a bountiful harvest. And it is into broken hearts that God, in love, plants His Word to save and prepare His people for some great work.

The apostle Paul said, "Now may our Lord Jesus Christ . . . who has loved us and given us everlasting consolation . . . establish you in every good word and work" (2 Thessalonians 2:16–17).

Who can describe or measure the love of God? When we read of God's justice, it is justice tempered with love. When we read of God's righteousness, it is righteousness founded on love. When we read of God's atonement for sin, it is atonement necessitated because of His love, provided by His love, finished by His love.

When we read about the resurrection of Christ, we see the miracle of

His love. When we read about the abiding presence of Christ, we know the power of His love. When we read about the return of Christ, we long for the fulfillment of His love.

No matter how black, dirty, shameful, or terrible our sin, God will forgive. We may be at the very gate of Hell itself, but He will be reaching out in everlasting love.

The Mighty One, will save;
He will rejoice over you with gladness,
He will quiet you with His love,
He will rejoice over you with singing. (Zephaniah 3:17)

CHAPTER 15

Everlasting Peace

Peace Promises

Ezekiel

I will make a covenant of peace with them, and it shall be . . . **everlasting**.

—Ezekiel 37:26

I KNOW MEN AND WOMEN WHO WOULD WRITE A CHECK FOR A MILLION DOLLARS IF THEY COULD FIND PEACE, BUT PEACE CANNOT BE BOUGHT. Millions search for what can only be found in Christ. And Satan does everything in his power to steer peace seekers away. He blinds them and bluffs them.

We talk of peace, lobby for it, and convene peace conferences, yet the world is heading toward anything but peace.

This is no different than in the days of the prophets. The ancient world was in upheaval. Many had given up hope for future peace. No wonder; they had turned to idols that could not speak or hear, much less lead them to peace. They had turned their backs on God. So He searched for a man who would bring the Word of God to His people, to declare His promise of peace, and He tapped Ezekiel on the shoulder for service in His name.

In every generation, God puts His hand on those He chooses to be His instruments. God's call must be a call, not a profession, which causes some of us to fear. We are afraid that God may call us into a work we don't want to do or that we do not feel equipped to do. But if God calls, He equips.

Ezekiel was such a man—faithful to God. He lived in exile in Babylon and faced tremendous opposition from deceptive prophets who preached a false hope of peace, saying that Israel would return to their land quicker than what was going to happen. "They have seduced My people, saying, 'Peace!' when there is no peace" (Ezekiel 13:10).

God had warned that judgment was coming if the people did not change their ways. They ignored Him and continued worshiping idols that could not lead them or save them.

But God will always have a remnant of people faithful to Him. "'When these days are over . . . I will accept you,' says the Lord GOD" (43:27).

The human race continues its futile search for peace in all the wrong places, placing its hope in governments, successes, or religions. This is what the Bible says concerning mankind's futility: "The way of peace they have not known" (Romans 3:17).

Today there is little personal, domestic, social, economic, or political peace anywhere. Why? Mankind has within it the seeds of suspicion, violence, hatred, and destruction.

Peace will not come to the world until Christ returns. "Do you suppose that I came to give peace on earth? I tell you, not at all, but rather division" (Luke 12:51). Jesus was not saying that He prevented peace; He was giving fair warning that His message would divide people. After all, who likes to be told they are sinners who must repent?

When Christ began His earthly ministry, He showed love, gave comfort, and brought healing. The people's response was to oppose Him, reject Him, arrest Him, and kill Him. This was a shocking blow to His disciples, so He said to the twelve, "These things I have spoken to you, that in Me you may have peace. In the world you will have tribulation; but be of good cheer, I have overcome the world" (John 16:33).

Jesus also revealed that a great war would come at the end of the age:

> "And you will hear of wars and rumors of wars. See that you are not troubled; for all these things must come to pass. . . . For nation will rise against nation, and kingdom against kingdom. And there will be famines, pestilences, and earthquakes in various places. All these are the beginning of sorrows." (Matthew 24:6–8)

That doesn't sound too peaceful, does it? So why does God allow it? So that the Gospel will be preached around the world as a witness to all the nations, "and then the end will come" (v. 14). I believe this is where we are today in God's great plan.

I can recall sitting in the visitors' gallery of London's House of Commons in 1954, watching the dramatic scene as the prime minister sat with the heads of government discussing what to do with the hydrogen bomb—often called the Hell bomb or the terror bomb. Many felt this weapon would bring about the destruction of the world.

Six decades have passed since then. Each generation has witnessed terrifying world events. The twenty-first century was inaugurated with the horrific 9/11 tragedy that set the whole world on edge. Today nations are in turmoil as governments struggle with how to defeat global terrorism. People are frantic, searching for solutions.

There is only one solution, and it is found in the righteous Ruler—the Man of peace. Jesus holds the key to man's problems, which are bound up in one little word—*sin*.

I have talked with people from all walks of life about how they deal with their fears. Some turn to alcohol; others turn to mystic religions and amusement. I say to them, "Come to Christ, He will overcome your fears. He will strengthen you to stand strong in the face of trials and disappointments." Paul understood this secret: "Therefore I take pleasure in infirmities, in reproaches, in needs, in persecutions, in distresses, for

Christ's sake. For when I am weak, then I am strong" (2 Corinthians 12:10). In the midst of cataclysmic events, there is peace that passes understanding.

Jesus knew that human nature was not going to change without a spiritual new birth. People think they want peace in the world, but what they really need is peace in their hearts. If that happened, there would be peace in the world as well.

Lasting peace is foreign to human thinking. God knew that the vast majority of the human race was never going to be converted to Him. Think about it. How many people do you brush shoulders with daily who are truly born again? In most cases the answer is "few." So we always have the potential that violence will break out in a home, in a community, or in the world.

What are we to do? We must first look within our darkened souls and get right with God. "We have peace with God through our Lord Jesus Christ" (Romans 5:1).

Jesus blesses those who proclaim the "gospel of peace" (Ephesians 6:15) and those who work for peace. "Blessed are the peacemakers" (Matthew 5:9). This does not mean pacifism but that we hope for peace, for Christ is peace. The Bible says, "And He came and preached peace to you who were afar off and to those who were near" (Ephesians 2:17).

Three kinds of peace are described in the Bible. First, there is a peace that you can have immediately—*peace with God* (Colossians 1:20). The greatest warfare going on in the world today is between man and God. It would be the greatest tragedy if I didn't tell you that unless you repent of your sins and receive Christ as your Savior, you are going to be lost—there will be no peace in Hell. The Bible says,

> But the wicked are like the troubled sea,
> When it cannot rest. (Isaiah 57:20)

It's not just head belief; it's heart belief too. We must bring everything to the cross, where the Lord Jesus Christ died for our sins; otherwise, "there is no peace . . . / For the wicked" (v. 21).

God made peace by the shedding of His blood. The war that exists between us and God can be over quickly, and the peace treaty will be signed in the blood of His Son Jesus Christ.

The second peace spoken of in the Bible is the *peace of God*. Everyone who knows the Lord can go through any problem—and face death—and still have the peace of God in his heart, for He makes it possible. "To be spiritually minded is life and peace" (Romans 8:6).

A psychiatrist once said he could not improve upon the apostle Paul's prescription for human worry. Paul said, "Be anxious for nothing, but in everything by prayer and supplication, with thanksgiving, let your requests be made known to God; and the peace of God, which surpasses all understanding, will guard your hearts and minds through Christ Jesus" (Philippians 4:6–7). The peace of God can be in our hearts—right now (Colossians 3:15). There is no human philosophy that can achieve such changes or provide such strength.

Christ promotes our inward peace by developing our spirits. "Now may the God of peace Himself sanctify you completely; and may your whole spirit, soul, and body be preserved blameless" (1 Thessalonians 5:23).

What a life! I know where I've come from. I know why I'm here. I know *where I am* going. His peace floods my heart and overwhelms my soul, even in the midst of despair!

A colleague who traveled frequently throughout the Middle East was in a car with some missionaries driving through the Jordanian desert, along the King's Highway, when a sandstorm blew up. They were on a mountain pass with low visibility. Though an experienced traveler, my friend said his knuckles were white until one of the missionaries said, "Don't worry. I've been this way before." They pulled off in a safe place and enjoyed a peaceful visit until the storm passed. That's what peace with God is like.

Even the birds know peace: The sea was beating against the rocks in huge, dashing waves. The lightning was flashing. The thunder was roaring. The wind was blowing. But the little bird was asleep in the crevice of the rock, its head tucked serenely under its wing, sound asleep. That is peace—to be at rest in the storm.

Jesus was asleep in the boat when a storm like that arose. The disciples were terrified and woke Him, "Lord, we will perish; save us!"

Jesus "said to the sea, 'Peace, be still!' And the wind ceased" (Mark 4:39).

In Christ, we can be at peace in the midst of the confusions, bewilderments, and perplexities of this life. The storm rages, but our hearts are at rest.

The third peace the Scripture mentions is *future peace*. A time is coming when the whole world will be at peace—it is a promise from God. But the storm will come first, and the world will be in utter despair.

If we do not understand true peace, we open ourselves up to deceit. One day a deceiver will appear on the world's stage and proclaim that he will bring peace to the world. He will tickle the ears of the people. He will convincingly perform acts that will awe the nations. Those who listen and follow him will go down with him.

An FBI agent once told my wife, "We spot counterfeits by studying the real thing." Likewise, how do we spot deceivers? By knowing the One who is real. He is Truth. Lies and deceit are in opposition to the truth. Oh, there may be hints of truth in a deceiver's dialogue, but genuine truth will arrest the fraud.

There is no question that the world is heading toward Armageddon. John wrote of the fiery red horse, "And it was granted to the one who sat on it to take peace from the earth" (Revelation 6:4). The earth will convulse as the judgment of God is unleashed, but peace will not come until the Prince of Peace returns.

And He is coming. One of these days the sky is going to break open, and the Lord will come back and bring His wonderful peace.

Imagine! There has been no world peace since Cain murdered Abel. But God has not left us in hopeless despair. He sent His prophets to proclaim the promise of peace. He sent the Lord Jesus, the Savior, who is the hope of peace.

> For unto us a Child is born,
> Unto us a Son is given;

And the government will be upon His shoulder.

And His name will be called . . .

Prince of Peace.

Of the increase of His government and peace

There will be no end. (Isaiah 9:6–7)

My colleagues George Beverly Shea and Cliff Barrows sang a song together that I always loved: *Jesus speaks peace to me.*[1] Study what the Bible says about the Source of peace; you will be blessed.

Jesus is the Author of peace. Jesus fills our hearts with peace. Jesus guides our way in peace. Jesus tells us to go in peace and depart in peace. Jesus gives us peace in trouble. Jesus gives us the fruit of peace. Jesus Himself is our peace. Jesus speaks peace. Jesus will rule in peace. And Jesus, in peace, will crush Satan.

Peace is a certainty. While Jesus did not leave a material inheritance to His disciples—all He had when He died was a robe—Jesus willed His followers something more valuable than gold. He willed them peace in spirit and peace eternal.

The world, however, cannot offer peace. It fights for peace, negotiates for peace, and maneuvers for peace, but it has none to give. So it remains restless.

A quiet revolution is going on in the world today. It has no fanfare, no media coverage, and no propaganda, yet it is changing the course of lives. It is restoring purpose and meaning as people of all races and nationalities are finding peace with God.

Now may the God of peace who brought up our Lord Jesus
from the dead, that great Shepherd of the sheep . . . make you
complete in every good work to do His will. (Hebrews 13:20–21)

KINGDOM WORSHIP FOREVER

Bow Down or Stand Up

DANIEL

King Nebuchadnezzar sent this message to the people of every race and nation and language throughout the world: . . .

"I want you all to know about the miraculous signs and wonders the Most High God has performed for me. . . .

His kingdom will last **forever.***"*

—DANIEL 4:1–3 NLT

THEY WERE FIFTEEN HUNDRED MILES FROM HOME. Who would know? Who would care?

God.

As young men, they had dedicated and committed themselves totally to Him.

Who are these young men? The Bible tells us that Daniel, along with his three friends Meshach, Shadrach, and Abed-Nego, had been chosen from the tribe of Judah to serve in the Babylonian king's royal court. King Nebuchadnezzar had conquered Jerusalem and had taken these Jewish youths captive. They were assertive and disciplined men, and they respectfully refused to eat from the king's table because the food had been offered to idols. They had purposed in their hearts (Daniel 1:8) that they would not go against the law of God, no matter what.

Nebuchadnezzar had become powerful and egotistical. So he built a statue to himself—a looming image, ninety feet high and nine feet wide, made of gold. He called his subjects from surrounding nations to come to the plain of Dura. Then he commanded that when the music played, the people were to bow down to worship the statue. "Whoever does not fall down and worship," he declared, "shall be cast immediately into the midst of a burning fiery furnace" (3:6).

False religion does not hesitate to use force. The Bible teaches that Satan is the god of this world. He is called the "prince of the power of the air" (Ephesians 2:2), and the "ruler of this world" (John 12:31), and he desires to take all the glory from God. He devises ways to do this through men and women.

Satan tried this in the wilderness with Jesus, insisting that Jesus bow down and worship him. He didn't, of course. Neither did He argue or debate. He simply declared, "It is written" (Matthew 4:4). He used the Word of God. That is why it is important for us to memorize passages in the Bible. Jesus used Scripture as a weapon against evil. It is God's Word that has authority and Holy Spirit power.

Jesus said to the devil, "You shall worship the LORD your God, and Him only you shall serve" (v. 10). He underscored it for his disciples: "No one can serve two masters" (6:24).

The three Hebrews found themselves between two masters, but not for long. They had a choice to make. They could have bowed down and avoided trouble, but that would have compromised their belief. They could have justified it as allegiance to government. They could have rationalized and said, "It is our duty to obey the king." But they didn't. They served a higher law—God's. So they refused to bow down.

These young men were staring persecution right in the face as they stood before the king. Nebuchadnezzar was puffed up with pride as he spoke about the great image, overlaid with gold, flashing in the sun. "I built it!" he said in outrage. It was an idol erected to his success and human glory. There was no thought of God's command, "Thou shalt have no other gods before me" (Exodus 20:3 KJV). The king didn't think about God at all. He bragged, "Look what I have built!"

Some of us say that also: "Look what I've done." "I have built this business." "I am a self-made man (or woman)." "I built this ranch." "I did this." "I did that." Satan calls upon people to bow down to pride, lust, and many other things. Man's success is among our many idols today.

Daily we are called to make choices. When it comes to whom or what we worship, we have two choices: bow to the things of this world and spiritually die, or bow down before the true God and live.

Shadrach, Meshach, and Abed-Nego could have stayed indoors that day. But that would have been cowardly. Instead, they had an opportunity to witness to thousands and seized the moment. These three Hebrew men refused to bow down. They stood up.

You might say they had a Joshua moment. Knowing the Scripture, they no doubt remembered Joshua's rally cry—to choose whom they would serve (Joshua 24:15). Whom will you serve, the true and living God? Or will you serve those things the devil brings across your path and the images that he places before you?

King Nebuchadnezzar was angry to learn that these men would not obey and bow. He reminded them of the penalty they would face, and he taunted them, "And who is the god who will deliver you from my hands?" (Daniel 3:15).

They boldly proclaimed, "Our God whom we serve is able to deliver us . . . and He will deliver us from your hand, O king. But if not, let it be known to you, O king, that we do not serve your gods, nor will we worship the gold image which you have set up" (vv. 17–18).

These young men of courage didn't know that God would deliver them. They had confidence that He *could*; but if not, He would be with them no matter what.

Why did they dare to face the rage of the infuriated tyrant? They saw Him who is invisible and were conscious of the glories that awaited them in the eternal kingdom of their God. Their faith in Him, their heavenly King, was unmovable. They had their sights not on earthly worship but on eternal worship.

Many believers today are living in situations like this, and the time is coming in our nation when we, too, may face such persecution. Oh, that we would be people who would say, "Our God will deliver us, but if not, we still refuse to worship the things of this world."

We must do as these young men: pre-decide, based on our faith in God, what our response will be. God said, "My Spirit shall not strive with man forever" (Genesis 6:3). There comes a point where, if we go beyond it, it is difficult to return. If we persist in bowing to the images of this world and rejecting the true and living God in the here and now, we will follow the devil to Hell in the hereafter. That is why the Bible says, "Do not love the world or the things in the world. If anyone loves the world, the love of the Father is not in him" (1 John 2:15).

We need to say either yes or no. But some of us say maybe. Some of us try to straddle the fence and live in both worlds, but Jesus will not compromise with us. The Gospel plan is all set. We must accept His Son if we are to enter His eternal kingdom. If your answer is not yes, then the choice is made.

When your trial comes—and it will if you are following Christ—act in the light of eternity. Do not judge the situation by the king's threat or by the heat of the fiery furnace, but by the everlasting God and the eternal life that awaits you.

It always costs something to follow Jesus Christ. Some years ago in a country where Christians were looked upon with suspicion and disfavor, a government leader said to me with an unscrupulous twinkle in his eye, "Christians seem to thrive under persecution. Perhaps we should prosper them, and they would disappear."

There is an underlying truth in this statement. Many rely on Christ when they have nothing to lean on except Him, but then they fall away when they climb the ladder of success. They think they can lean on their own power and authority, forgetting about Jesus. They just don't have time for Him anymore.

No one desires persecution, which can come in many forms, but may we be people empowered by the Lord to stand strong when those times come.

Throughout the world today there are people who are enduring cruelties because of their Christian faith. We must pray for them, and for ourselves, that in our own dying hour God will give us grace to endure until the end, anticipating the certainty of His glory to come. Whatever the cost, we must obey.

Whether in life or in death, faithfulness to God brings Him glory. Shadrach, Meschach, and Abed-Nego exhibited their faith in God as they walked calmly toward death. It was clear that they did not fear Nebuchadnezzar; their confidence was in God.

When they were bound and cast into the fiery furnace, the king stood back so that he wouldn't be burned. But when he looked into the furnace, he was astonished at what he saw. "Look . . . I see four men loose, walking in the midst of the fire; and they are not hurt, and the form of the fourth is like the Son of God" (Daniel 3:25).

You see, God is with His people in the fiery furnace. He is with His people in times of temptation, trouble, and trial, for nothing "shall be able to separate us from the love of God" (Romans 8:39).

Shadrach, Meshach, and Abed-Nego certainly learned that truth. When the king ordered them taken out, they emerged unharmed; not a hair was singed, and the "fire had no power" over them. Not even their clothes smelled of smoke (Daniel 3:27).

Nebuchadnezzar spoke, saying, "Blessed be the God of Shadrach, Meshach, and Abed-Nego . . . they have frustrated the king's word, and yielded their bodies, that they should not serve nor worship any god except their own God! . . . There is no other God who can deliver like this." (vv. 28–29)

What a change took place in the mighty Nebuchadnezzar that day. None of his gods could perform such a miracle. These young men dared to look death in the face in the name of their God, and what glory was given to Him as a result.

You may ask, "Why didn't God rescue Jesus from the cross?" Jesus willingly went to the cross to rescue us. The night before Christ died, He bowed down to the Father in submission, and the next day He was lifted up as the sacrifice for the sins of man. He was slain on the cross and then buried. Then He emerged from the tomb victorious over death, so that we may enjoy the riches of His everlasting kingdom as we worship Him throughout eternity.

And the Lord will deliver me from every evil work
and preserve me for His heavenly kingdom. To Him
be glory forever and ever. (2 Timothy 4:18)

CHAPTER 17

His Name Is Eternal

Majoring on the Minors

THE TWELVE

For all people walk each in the name of his god,
But we will walk in the name of the LORD our God
Forever and ever.

—MICAH 4:5

A POLITICIAN ONCE TOLD ME THAT HE READ THE NEWSPAPER ONLY IF HIS NAME WAS IN IT. The names of politicians come and go, but the Name that is eternal is the One worthy of our attention.

These last twelve books of the Old Testament, collectively known as the Minor Prophets, are sometimes called the Twelve. In them we see the name and voice of almighty God questioned, examined, and exalted.

Preceding these twelve writers, the prophet Isaiah wrote of "the High and Lofty One / Who inhabits eternity, whose name is Holy" (57:15).

The prophet Daniel declared,

> Blessed be the name of God forever and ever,
> For wisdom and might are His. (2:20)

Studying names and numbers in Scripture is boring to some, but they carry a great and interesting significance. Here we consider the number twelve—an eternal number.

From Genesis to Revelation we learn of the twelve patriarchs, twelve sons, twelve tribes of Israel, twelve judges, twelve gates, twelve stones, twelve fruits, twelve angels, twelve apostles, twelve stars, and a heavenly city twelve thousand furlongs square. The Bible also tells us that after Jesus' birth, nothing more is revealed about Him until He reaches the age of twelve, when His first words on earth are recorded. Jesus told those who had been looking for Him, "I must be about My Father's business" (Luke 2:49). This number is also foreshadowed when twelve thousand from each of the twelve tribes of Israel will be saved to once again evangelize the world in the last days.

His prophetic word, though, has been with the human race from the beginning. Anticipation builds as the Minor Prophets bring the Old Testament to a close so that the New Testament can begin revealing the wonderful truth that "eternity" is coming to earth. His name is Jesus.

These Minor Prophets are not so named because they are in training or because they are of less value than prophets such as Isaiah or Ezekiel. Nor are the twelve books minor in message. They are minor in terms of brevity only. Each little book is no more than just a few pages, but they are power-packed messages from men whom God appointed and called to deliver His warnings of judgments and His ever-faithful invitation to Israel and its neighbors, saying, "Return to Me." They provide an important study for those who truly desire to understand the end times—which should include all believers because these words speak of things eternal.

These prophets, whose lifetimes spanned several hundred years of Israel's history, warned of pending doom because of the people's grotesque sin against God. Israel had been scattered among the nations in judgment for disobeying God's Word. The remnant left in Jerusalem remained under the sacrificial system that required twelve animal sacrifices (one for each tribe of Israel) in payment for sin.

While there is much to cover concerning the historical and future prophesies of Israel and the nations, I would like to shine a spotlight on the marvelous invitations to salvation found in these little books. While biblical prophecy does predict what is to come, the most important aspect is to sound a warning, giving people the chance to consider their ways and repent. This is the work of evangelism. While evangelists proclaim the Good News of Jesus Christ, we must also proclaim the judgment that is coming and what to expect when the Gospel is rejected.

The tender mercies of God call out to lost souls. The invitation is rich in God's eternal love for mankind. And these prophetic voices engage in conversation with those opposed to God's ways, who ignore the patient nature of God. He sends out His spokesmen to proclaim the remedy: return to the Lord with rejoicing. It is this saving thread that is woven through these prophecies in a way that helps us to see the heart of God for His people.

I have known some who have been saved through the study of these passages. While each prophecy carries its own specific message, all remain anchored to a trinity of thought: remember, return, and rejoice. Most of these books begin with some variation of "Now the word of the Lord came to . . ." The prophets were God's examples to the world of what He wanted His people, the Israelites, to be—God's light in a dark world. They will be someday.

The prophets also wrote that the Word of God went forth (Isaiah 55:11). What were these messages?

HOSEA: REAPING SIN'S CONSEQUENCES

Hosea preached the dangerous consequences of sin. When Israel was at peace, their prosperity grew, but so did their iniquity. They were immersed in idolatry. Israel had played the harlot—loving other gods. They loved shame more than honor. As God told Hosea, "My people are bent on backsliding from Me" (Hosea 11:7).

There's not too much preaching today about backsliders, those who once followed God but then fell away from faith, grieving the Holy Spirit by their sin and coldness of heart. Proverbs tells us that "the backslider in heart will be filled with his own ways" (14:14). People have told me that their years of wandering brought them much grief and heartache, and it often took a tragedy to bring them back to God.

The Lord said:

> My people are being destroyed
>   because they don't know me. . . .
> They do not cry out to me with sincere hearts. . . .
> They have planted the wind
>   and will [reap] the whirlwind. (Hosea 4:6; 7:14; 8:7
>   NLT)

This happens today. Why? Sometimes faith isn't real; some claim to know Christ but never commit to Him. For others, temptation lures them into sin, and they do not rely on God's power to resist. Whatever the reason, backsliders compromise their faith, causing unbelievers to mock the Gospel. The Bible says, "Beware, brethren, lest there be in any of you an evil heart of unbelief in departing from the living God" (Hebrews 3:12).

Evil encompasses more than murder and immorality; unbelief in the Lord Jesus Christ is the greatest evil. God revealed this to His people and told them that they had become as vile as the gods they worshiped (Hosea 9:10). The more He called to them, the farther away they wandered.

But the Lord's relentless invitation goes beyond all human comprehension to save.

> My heart is torn within me,
> and my compassion overflows. . . .
> For I am God and not a mere mortal.
> I am the Holy One living among you. . . .
> You must acknowledge no God but me,
> for there is no other savior. (11:8–9; 13:4 NLT)

Hosea contrasts sin's consequences to the reaping of righteousness and says,

> Plant the good seeds of righteousness,
> and you will harvest a crop of love.
> Plow up the hard ground of your hearts . . .
> that he may come
> and shower righteousness upon you. (10:12 NLT)

Then the Lord appeals to them with a promise: "I will . . . transform the Valley of Trouble into a gateway of hope" (2:15 NLT).

Only the Lord could love deeply enough to offer hope in a call to repentance. He also tells them how to respond to His invitation:

> Return . . . to the LORD your God,
> for your sins have brought you down. . . .
> Say to him,
> "Forgive all our sins and graciously receive us." . . .
> The LORD says,
> "Then I will heal you of your faithlessness;
> my love will know no bounds." (14:1–4 NLT)

Only hardened hearts can miss the Lord's compassion:

> O Israel, stay away from idols!
> I am the one who answers your prayers and cares
> for you. . . .
> All your fruit comes from me. (vv. 8–9 NLT)

This is a glorious invitation to those wandering far from Him—repent of sin and reap righteousness, for "the LORD is His memorable name" (12:5).

JOEL: REPENTING OF SIN

When Joel came on the scene he preached a message of repentance:

> Sound an alarm! . . .
> For the day of the LORD is coming. (Joel 2:1)

Swarms of locusts had left the land desolate, but the prophet predicted that much worse would come. Many today say, "Well, there's no reason to dread the 'day of the Lord,'" but they had better look again. "The day of the LORD is an awesome, terrible thing" (v. 11 NLT) because this is the Day of Judgment.

Yet a loving invitation goes out for God's people to repent:

> "Turn to me now, while there is time.
> Give me your hearts. . . .
> Don't tear your clothing in your grief,
> but tear your hearts instead."
> Return to the LORD your God,
> for he is . . .
> filled with unfailing love.

He is eager to relent and not punish. (vv. 12–13 NLT)

The Lord promised to restore the years the locust had destroyed through this remarkable invitation:

Whoever calls on the name of the LORD
Shall be saved. (v. 32)

Whoever is a wonderfully big word; it speaks of the grace of God and His invitation that extends to all people. Paul quoted from this passage in his epistle to the Romans: "For there is no distinction between Jew and Greek, for the same Lord over all is rich to all who call upon Him" (10:12).

Christianity is centered on the Gospel that brings comfort, the assurance that God will forgive sin. But an unbelieving world sees Christianity as a Gospel of crisis because it boldly proclaims that the world's days are numbered. Every cemetery testifies to this. The Bible teaches that life is only a vapor that appears for a moment and then vanishes (James 4:14). This is why God calls out to the nations of the world to get right with Him.

History will someday come to an end, rendering the world's system, dominated by evil, a total failure. Wickedness in every form will cease: hatred, greed, jealousy, war, and death. This "day of the Lord" will be glorious, when He comes to bring peace to the "whosoevers."

Repent, and "praise the name of the LORD your God . . . / And my people shall never be put to shame" (Joel 2:26).

AMOS: REJECTING SIN

Now Amos comes along with a warning about the people's rejection of the Lord. He was a shepherd in a barren and rocky place called Tekoa. He was not cultured or clever, but he had a burning and flaming message.

Israel was a divided nation, like Korea is today. Both kingdoms (ten tribes in the north and two in the south) were at peace and prospering.

Outwardly everything seemed to be well, but God, who sees the heart, saw the cancer within. They had security, comfort, and wealth, but their spiritual health was in decline. In the midst of this affluence and arrogance, God called Amos. He left his plowing and headed into battle.

Well, you may say, the Bible records that the people were worshiping. Let's look at their worship and the message the Lord gave His prophet to deliver:

> I hate, I despise your feast days,
> And I do not savor your sacred assemblies. . . .
> Take away from Me the noise of your songs. . . .
> Woe to you who are at ease in Zion. . . .
> Who sing idly to the sound of stringed instruments.
>   (Amos 5:21, 23; 6:1, 5)

They worshiped outwardly but disobeyed inwardly. They were indifferent to sin within the assembly. They had ignored God's law and intimidated the prophets not to preach the truth; they did not want their dull consciences to be disturbed. God loathed their services and had no use for their festivals and rich offerings. They had rejected Him, and He rejected their phony worship in every way:

> Hear this, you who swallow up the needy,
> And make the poor of the land fail. . . .
> "Behold, the days are coming," says the Lord God,
> "That I will send a famine on the land,
> Not a famine of bread,
> Nor a thirst for water,
> But of hearing the words of the Lord." (8:4, 11–12)

There is a great famine today of God's Word. We hear the Word but don't feed on it. Can you imagine bringing food into a refugee camp and the people looking at it but not partaking? We need to be hungry for truth. We have not only lost the way in calling out sin in the community; we have also lost the address in calling out to God.

America has become obsessed with financial success. Cheating and lying have become normal business practices. Moral shortcuts have become acceptable behavior. Americans are preoccupied with pleasure and amusement. As the twenty-first century approached, we hoped for peace, but we had hardly opened the cover of a new millennium when our country got a wake-up call, and we failed to heed it.

Well, Israel got a wake-up call with a powerful message from Amos because of her rejection of God. As the deafening alarm shrieked through the sinful land, the prophet sent out the call:

> Prepare to meet your God, O Israel! . . .
> Seek good and not evil,
> That you may live. (4:12, 5:14)

How do you prepare to meet God? Repent of sin. Instead of rejecting Him, receive Him; for "the LORD God of hosts is His Name" (4:13).

OBADIAH: READY YOURSELF

Obadiah preached, "Get ready!"

This, the shortest book in the Old Testament, records the judgment against the people of Edom, the descendants of Esau.

Do you remember the terrible conflict between the sons of Isaac—Esau and Jacob? They were twin brothers whose lives were intertwined by birth yet embattled by heritage. This conflict still rages and will until the end. Esau sold his birthright to satisfy a momentary desire. Throughout Scripture, Esau symbolizes the world's wicked system. The birthright, given to Jacob, represents those who return to the Lord.

Obadiah proclaimed God's invitation to Edom with urgency.

"Get ready, everyone! . . .
"You have been deceived by your own pride
    because you live in a rock fortress
    and make your home high in the mountains.
'Who can ever reach us way up here?'
    you ask boastfully.
But . . .
I will bring you crashing down,"
    says the LORD. (vv. 1, 3–4 NLT)

Once again we see the Lord's warning: repent, or get ready for judgment. The Lord reminded the people of Edom of their sin against their kin when they rejoiced over Judah's destruction. God would have blessed them, but they robbed their relatives and left them defenseless, so God declared His judgment: "As you have done, it shall be done to you" (v. 15).

This is a crucial message to Israel's ancestors, the descendants of Esau and the cousins of Jacob. The land of Edom is in present-day Jordan, where the magnificent red rock city of Petra is located. The Bible tells us that in the last days, people will be so terrified that they will escape to the mountains, thinking that the Lord will not find them and bring them to His judgment seat. But no one can escape the judgment of almighty God. It is better to "get ready" and be prepared than to run and be caught by the Lord's hand.

Return to Him, for this land has been promised to Israel, and one day its people will return home (v. 20). God's eternal promises will come to pass. Judgment will come to the mountains of Esau, "and the kingdom shall be the LORD's" (v. 21).

JONAH: REBELLING IN SIN

Jonah is one who thought he could escape from the Lord—he found out differently. He was called to preach to rebellious Nineveh, but instead he rebelled against God's call. This miraculous story proves that God's eyes are everywhere and that He devises retribution and punishment to bring about eternal blessing in response to repentance.

Jonah was called to preach God's Word, but in a very different way from other prophets who preached to Israel.

Jonah resented the fact that God was sending him to the "great city" (Jonah 1:2), the capital of Israel's pagan neighbor, Assyria. He didn't believe the people of Nineveh deserved God's salvation. So he did the very thing he was called to preach against—he disobeyed God and did what was in his heart.

This epic story reveals that before God could use Jonah, Jonah first had to humble himself and repent. Only then would God use him to evangelize the entire city.

The prophet left God's path and boarded a ship. When a ferocious storm nearly capsized the vessel, Jonah, who admitted to the crew that he was running from God, was thrown overboard, and the storm immediately ceased. Because of his rebellion against the Lord, Jonah found God's judgment in the belly of a big fish, and he lived to tell about it! You might say that Jonah had an attitude adjustment before he was coughed up on shore three days later, repentant and ready to go to Nineveh.

Perhaps the seamen who threw Jonah overboard spread the story of his "resurrection" from the sea, for in the providence of God, word spread that the prophet was in town. The king was so overcome by Jonah's message that he himself called for complete repentance. "Cry mightily to God," the king of Nineveh pleaded with his people. "Let every one turn from his evil way and from the violence that is in his hands. Who can tell if God will turn and relent, and turn away from His fierce anger, so that we may not perish?" (3:8–9).

When God heard the cries, He relented of His judgment and brought salvation to the city. Jonah's response is stunning; he withdrew in anger and sulked. He could not rejoice in the outpouring of God's mercy and kindness to Israel's enemy. Oh, how vital it is for those who preach the Gospel and those who pray for revival to have their hearts right with God.

God reprimanded Jonah and, in graciousness, expressed His pity and love for those wandering in an evil world drowning in sin. This is yet another demonstration of the long arm of God's salvation extended to those who turn from rebellion and receive the Lord's mighty message of forgiveness.

MICAH: REQUIRING OBEDIENCE

Micah's message was a declaration of what the Lord requires of His people:

> Attention! Let all the people of the world listen! . . .
> The Sovereign LORD is making accusations against
>   you. . . .
> Look! The LORD is coming!
>   He leaves his throne in heaven
>   and tramples the heights of the earth. (Micah 1:2–3 NLT)

Well, this is quite a heralding from the prophet. The lands of the nations were polluted with idols; corruption permeated every facet of life. The Lord had been ignored.

Sound familiar? That is why Micah's warning still resonates so strongly today.

First, the sobering news. When Jesus returns, He will find a polluted land filled with corrupt people, and He will require an accounting on the day He judges each individual. All outside of Christ will answer for what they've done and what they've said; even their thoughts and motives. This is why Micah goes right to the heart of evil:

> Woe to those who devise iniquity,
> And work out evil on their beds!
> At morning light they practice it,
> Because it is in the power of their hand. (2:1)

The prophet calls out the rulers, holding them accountable for not knowing and not doing justice:

> "You who hate good and love evil. . . .
> He will even hide His face from them. . . .
> The [false] prophets
> Who make my people stray;
> Who chant "Peace" . . .
> But who prepare war against him. . . .
> "There is no answer from God." (3:2, 4, 5, 7)

Now for the glorious news: When Jesus returns, all evil will be destroyed. Weapons of war will no longer be needed.

We sigh with relief when we hear this eternal promise:

> They shall beat their swords into plowshares,
> And their spears into pruning hooks;
> Nation shall not lift up sword against nation,
> Neither shall they learn war anymore. (4:3)

For the first time in the history of mankind, there will be no war.

Micah contrasts the evil rulers and false prophets of his time with an invitation concerning the coming Messiah.

> Out of [Bethlehem] shall come forth to Me
> The One to be Ruler in Israel,
> Whose goings forth are from of old,
> From everlasting. . . .
>
> For now He shall be great
> To the ends of the earth;
> And this One shall be peace. . . .

That you may know the righteousness of the LORD.
(5:2–5; 6:5)

Micah declared what the Lord requires of His people:

To do what is right, to love mercy,
and to walk humbly with . . . God. (6:8 NLT)

In addition, he says, those who are wise will listen and recognize His name (v. 9).

In the majesty of the name of the LORD . . .
They shall abide. (5:4)

NAHUM: REVENGING EVIL

Nahum preached the message of revenge on evil. My wife, Ruth, wrote a book many years ago titled *Clouds Are the Dust of His Feet*, based on this little prophetic book. She loved Nahum's description of God stirring the clouds.

This prophet was called on by God to give another message to Nineveh. One hundred fifty years had passed since Jonah's citywide revival, and the people had fallen back into sin. As part of the nation of Assyria, Nineveh was also a constant threat to Israel. And God was angry about both.

It takes a great deal to stir God's anger—but when it happens, it is holy anger because He is pure and righteous. When the Bible tells us that God "is slow to anger" (Nahum 1:3), it simply means that He is patient beyond man's capability. Yet Nahum preached that God would take revenge on evil. "[He] will not at all acquit the wicked" (v. 3).

History often reflects that the wicked stay wicked. Who are the wicked? Those who break the law of God—and we have all broken God's law. We must not think that we get away with anything. Sin will bring us to repentance or retribution. When His anger is stirred, He often uses the power of nature to demonstrate His pending doom:

> The LORD has His way
> In the whirlwind and in the storm,
> And the clouds are the dust of His feet. . . .
> The earth heaves at His presence. (vv. 3–5)

So the storm clouds are swift, as holy feet stir up the dust of anger.

Every time the spiritual barometer of Israel and Judah went down, God raised up a storm in the form of a prophet, a message, and an invitation. This is why Nahum was now on the scene, bringing God's judgment call. Loving parents will warn their children before administering punishment for disobedience. God will do no less.

History reveals that the Lord had been merciful to Nineveh repeatedly.

> The LORD is good,
> A stronghold in the day of trouble;
> And He knows those who trust in Him. (v. 7)

God had also been patient. He had sent His salvation to the people and had warned them not to turn back to sin—but they did. So God instructed His prophet to say,

> The LORD has given a command concerning you:
> "Your name shall be perpetuated no longer. . . .
> I will dig your grave,
> For you are vile." (v. 14)

After such condemnation the Lord sent comfort to Israel, assuring them that Assyria would no longer hover over them. Judah had lived in fear of Assyria's continual attacks from the mountains. So the Lord comforted them, contrasting the movement of His feet on the clouds in anger to the consolation of the feet that carry the good news.

> Behold, on the mountains
> The feet of him who brings good tidings,
> Who proclaims peace! . . .
> Perform your vows.
> For the wicked one shall no more pass through you;
> He is utterly cut off. (v. 15)

God wanted them to remember His revenge on evil and to stir up their hearts for the sake of His great name.

HABAKKUK: REVIVING THE WORK

Habakkuk preached woe and prayed for revival. God does not owe us anything. We have no right to expect anything from Him other than His judgment. Yet He still gives us grace—His undeserved favor.

Habakkuk was perplexed as to why God was withholding punishment for Israel's lawlessness. The Lord said to him,

> Look among the nations and watch—
> Be utterly astounded!
> For I will work a work in your days. . . .
> For indeed I am raising up the Chaldeans,
> A bitter and hasty nation
> Which marches through the breadth of the earth,
> To possess dwelling places that are not theirs. . . .
> Their judgment and their dignity proceed from
>   themselves. (Habakkuk 1:5–7)

Now when the Bible says that God raises up evil, it does not mean that He puts evil in the hearts of people to do wrong, for He is not capable of evil. But He permits evil because doing so reveals man's heart.

The prophet was distraught to think God would send one of Israel's worst enemies, the Chaldeans—more wicked than Israel—to come against them. But Habakkuk accepted God's astonishing pronouncement and praised Him:

> Are You not from everlasting? . . .
> O Rock, You have marked them for correction.
> You are of purer eyes than to behold evil,
> And cannot look on wickedness. (vv. 12-13)

God comforted His prophet with a revelation that He would also punish the Chaldeans because it was in their heart to come against God's people. Then the Lord issued five "woes" that echo still today (2:6-19):

- Woe to him who increases his wealth by extortion.
- Woe to him who ensures his security by exploiting others.
- Woe to him who sheds innocent blood.
- Woe to him who brings shame on his neighbor.
- Woe to him who worships idols.

When Habakkuk realized that God meant business, he prayed for revival:

> O LORD, I have heard Your speech and was afraid;
> O LORD, revive Your work. . . .
> In the midst of the years make it known;
> In wrath remember mercy. (3:2)

Habakkuk rehearsed the graciousness of the Lord. When our trust begins to waver, we must trust Him more and remember what He has done for us in the past. God will keep all of His promises; eternity will prove it.

The prophet's remarkable prayer was a sermon to the people:

> Was it in anger, LORD, that you struck the rivers
>> and parted the sea? . . .
>> No, you were sending your chariots of salvation! . . .
> You went out to rescue your chosen people,
>> to save your anointed ones. . . .
>> I will be joyful in the God of my salvation!
>>> (vv. 8–13, 18 NLT)

Habakkuk declared his trust in the Lord to do right and invited others to remember God's mercy and abiding love, for *He is the Eternal One.*

ZEPHANIAH: REJOICING IN FORGIVENESS

Zephaniah preached, rejoicing in God's forgiveness. He exhorted God's people not to delay repentance. Act now! Don't wait! This is yet another of God's compelling invitations to mankind.

> Gather before judgment begins,
>> before your time to repent is blown away like chaff.
> Act now, before the fierce fury of the LORD falls. . . .
> Seek the LORD, all who are humble. . . .
> Seek to do what is right. . . .
>
> Perhaps even yet the LORD will protect you.
>> (Zephaniah 2:2–3 NLT)

God had delivered a blowing prophecy to His people through the prophet, and Zephaniah did not have to guess what was about to happen. Israel, God's special possession (Malachi 3:17 NLT), had defiled His very name:

> "They claim to follow the LORD,
>   but then they worship Molech, too.
> And I will destroy those who used to worship me
>   but now no longer do. . . ."

> "I will punish the leaders and princes of Judah
>   and all those following pagan customs.

> "On that day," says the LORD,
>   "a cry of alarm will come. . . .

> "I will search . . .
>   to punish those who sit complacent in their sins."
>   (Zephaniah 1:5–6, 8, 10, 12 NLT)

Though these prophecies are targeted to times and places, we must not let the eternal truths escape us. This condition is present today. Blending religions is nothing new, but Christianity is not a religion—it is faith in the one true God. However, there is a great movement taking place involving people who call themselves Christians mixing with world religions. This practice is gaining acceptance—but not with God.

A famous Hollywood actress and Golden Globe winner considers herself a Buddhist while claiming an abiding belief in the traditional God. Others say, "I like the gentle Jesus, but I don't care for a judging God." The truth is they are one in the same. God is one, and faith in God cannot be blended or mixed with anything. People may believe that they can "mix it up," but God will one day "shake all nations" (Haggai 2:7), and all that does not glorify Him will become desolate.

The day is coming when every nation and all peoples will worship the one true God. Those in rebellion will regret their rejection of Him, but then it will be too late. That's why Zephaniah said with urgency, "Act now!"

God calls out for repentance, for He will judge all those who are against Him. Then He will bring singing out of groaning and giving out of greed. The Lord will remove His hand of judgment, and He, the King, will live among us! This promise is our anchor in this life.

This message brought great hope and joy to the people as Zephaniah proclaimed,

> The LORD your God in your midst,
> The Mighty One, will save;
> He will rejoice over you with gladness,
> He will quiet you with His love,
> He will rejoice over you with singing. (Zephaniah 3:17)

On that day, the Lord promises to gather the redeemed and bring them home, and "they shall trust in the name of the LORD" (v. 12).

HAGGAI: REBUILDING THE HOUSE

Haggai proclaimed that it was time to rebuild the Lord's temple, which had been destroyed by the Babylonians. Repentance always brings renewal, so the prophet stirred up the people to get their minds off of themselves and pay attention to the things of the Lord. They had been sowing and reaping while the temple lay in ruins. Speaking for the Lord, he urged them, "Consider your ways. . . . and build the temple. . . . My house that is in ruins" (Haggai 1:7–9).

People by nature build, tear down, and rebuild. We build our hopes, get disappointed, and then search for renewed hope. That is why we are fond of New Year's resolutions. They are very popular in our culture today, though most are seldom kept. We get busy; we forget; we fail. Making resolutions, though, at least forces us into a moment of honesty about our need to change.

The Bible tells us to examine ourselves before the Lord. When we do this with sincerity, the Lord reveals where we fall short. This turns us back to God and helps us realize that we are incapable of living lives pleasing to Him apart from His help day by day, hour by hour.

Here in the book of Haggai, we see the prophet take inventory, you might say, and he reminds the people that everything they have belongs to the Lord. Haggai points out that they are busy making themselves look good instead of the Lord. Faith in God calls for building from the inside out. There is no sense in working on the outside if the inside is rotten. The message was that they were building on their own works and forgetting the Lord.

The Lord reminded the people of the former splendor of the Temple and said, "I will shake all the nations, and the treasures of all the nations will be brought to this Temple. I will fill this place with glory. . . . The silver is mine, and the gold is mine. . . . The future glory of this Temple will be greater than its past glory" 2:7–9 NLT).

Haggai makes no apologies for the repetition in proclaiming the Word of the Lord: consider, consider, consider.

Have you taken inventory lately? Have you considered where you stand with God? Return to the Lord and consider Him—the One who gives you everything. Build on His foundation. "And in this place," the Lord says, "I will bring peace" (v. 9 NLT).

ZECHARIAH: REASSURING THE REMNANT

Zechariah's message to the people is one of reassurance. There are great days ahead for repentant Israel when the Lord "whistle[s] for them"

(Zechariah 10:8) to gather in this oh-so-small land someday—a land that has been the center of attention throughout history. The nations of the world will bow their knees to the Lord. There will be no more distractions, no more backsliding, and no more idol worship, for all things will be engraved with "HOLINESS TO THE LORD" (14:20).

This is the most prophetic of the twelve books of the Minor Prophets, in the sense of speaking about the future. Zechariah sends out God's call to repentance and then proceeds to proclaim the many glorious promises from the Lord, renewing hope in the coming Messiah and giving assurance that the Lord will take possession of "His inheritance in the Holy Land" (2:12).

By the Word of the Lord, Zechariah rehearsed for the people their oppressive history so they would not forget the patience of the Lord. "Your ancestors refused to listen to this message. They stubbornly turned away and put their fingers in their ears to keep from hearing. They made their hearts as hard as stone" (7:11–12 NLT).

This is reminiscent of the story a youth minister told as he stood before a large group of teenagers and taught the Scripture. One of the boys in the back of the room sat with his fingers in his ears and his eyes closed. At the end of the meeting, the minister asked him why. The young man said, "My parents made me come, but I don't have to listen."

It is hard for a believer in Christ to imagine such resistance, but the Lord told His people, and tells us today,

> Call on My name,
> And I will answer. (13:9)

Ears that are shielded from God's voice have no hope.

For those who do hear and respond according to His command, God grants His assurance that they belong to Him. "Many nations will join themselves to the LORD . . . and they, too, will be my people" (2:11 NLT).

This book is filled with hope for today and for eternity. Zechariah says,

> Look, your king is coming to you.
> He is righteous and victorious. . . .
> On that day the LORD their God will rescue his
> people. . . .
> They will sparkle in his land
> like jewels in a crown. (9:9, 16 NLT)

If you haven't prepared in this life to meet God in eternity, open up your ears and ask Him to engrave your heart with His wonderful name. And the Lord will be King over all the earth. "On that day there will be one LORD—his name alone will be worshiped" (14:9 NLT).

MALACHI: RETURN TO ME

Malachi preached reverence to the name of the Lord and sent out the repeated call: "Return to Me." The Lord rebuked His people for not listening and said,

> A son honors his father,
> And a servant his master.
> If then I am the Father,
> Where is My honor?
> And if I am a Master,
> Where is My reverence? (Malachi 1:6)

This prophet didn't flinch in proclaiming God's entire word, exposing people's motives. God set the record straight when He revealed that they had despised and profaned His name through their empty sacrifices and disobedience. He called out:

> For I am the LORD, I do not change. . . .
> Return to Me. (3:6–7)

God is the same yesterday, today, and tomorrow, and we see clearly that His invitation is the same. And because He is unchanging, He is utterly trustworthy and faithful. We see the Lord's declaration all through Malachi's prophecy:

> My name shall be great among the Gentiles. . . . (1:11)
> My name is to be feared among the nations. . . . (1:14)
> Give glory to My name. . . . (2:2)
> [Be] reverent before My name. . . . (2:5)
> And . . . meditate on [My] name. (3:16)

This is a wonderful ending to the prophecy because it speaks of eternity in Heaven if your name is written there. "Whosoever will" is you and me (Revelation 22:17 KJV). You can have a tender and responsive heart or a stony and stubborn heart. You can be the apple of God's eye or a thorn bush that burns in the fire. You can be a jewel in the hand of God or you can try fleeing to the rocks—but you cannot hide from Him.

Malachi reveals,

> Then those who feared the LORD spoke to one
>   another,
> And the LORD listened and heard them;
> So a book of remembrance was written before Him.
>   (Malachi 3:16)

Then the prophecy draws to a close, as it opened, with God's love.

But to you who fear My name
The Sun of Righteousness shall arise
With healing in His wings. (4:2)

Do not turn a deaf ear to these prophecies, but return to the Son of the Righteous and eternal God who created you, and to the One who will save you—His name is Jesus.

Behold, the Man whose name is the BRANCH! . . .
"The LORD is one,"
And His name one. (Zechariah 6:12; 14:9)

THE NEW TESTAMENT

CHAPTER 18

ETERNAL PRAYER ANSWERED

Stray or Pray

MATTHEW

After this manner therefore pray. . . .
For thine is the kingdom, and the power, and
*the glory, **for ever**. Amen.*

—MATTHEW 6:9, 13 KJV

SECULARISM RULES THE DAY. The world is being carried on a rushing torrent that is sweeping out of control. Only one power can redeem the course of events, and that is the power of prayer.

To whom shall we pray? To the Source of the power.

Someone has said that "a nation cannot keep its freedom without the aid of almighty God." And prayer opens the gates of eternity to sinners saved by grace.

Uniting in prayer to the gods of this world will avail nothing. A clear demonstration of this is the story of Elijah and the prophets of Baal. Elijah said to the people,

> "How long will you falter between two opinions? If the LORD is God, follow Him; but if Baal, follow him." But the people answered him not a word. Then Elijah said to the people, "I alone am left a prophet of the LORD; but Baal's prophets are four hundred and fifty men." (1 Kings 18:21–22)

Elijah challenged the idol worshipers to prepare a sacrifice to Baal, and he would prepare a sacrifice to God. "Then you call on the name of your gods," he said, "and I will call on the name of the LORD; and the God who answers by fire, He is God" (v. 24).

The people prayed from morning until evening, "'O Baal, hear us!' But there was no voice; no one answered" (v. 26). The people cried in anguish. Then Elijah gathered them around and prepared the altar. He filled the trench around the altar with water three times so that no human effort could be credited for the miracle that would take place.

Then Elijah prayed,

> "LORD God of Abraham, Isaac, and Israel, let it be known this day that You are God. . . . I have done all these things at Your word. Hear me, O LORD . . . that this people may know that You are the LORD God. . . ."
>
> Then the fire of the LORD fell and consumed the burnt sacrifice . . . and it licked up the water that was in the trench. (vv. 36–38)

Dr. Donald Grey Barnhouse once said, "I am not so sure that I believe in the 'power of prayer,' but I do believe in the power of the Lord who answers prayer."[1] This was dramatically demonstrated in Elijah's day. The Bible tells us that the people fell on their faces and proclaimed, "The LORD, He is God!" (v. 39).

The gods of this world will not answer prayer offered in their names because the gods are made by human hands. They cannot see, they cannot touch, they cannot hear, they cannot speak, they cannot comfort, they cannot deliver, and they cannot save. But from one end of the Bible to the other, and throughout history, we find the record of those who turned the tide of history through prayers offered in the mighty name of God. He hears. He answers. He saves.

King Hezekiah prayed when his city was threatened by invading armies, and the nation was spared for another generation. The king had prayed and exalted the Almighty "that all the kingdoms of the earth may know that You are the LORD God, You alone" (2 Kings 19:19).

Daniel prayed three times a day for power to remain true to God (Daniel 6:13). Jesus prayed at the tomb of Lazarus so that the people would believe (John 11:41-42). Paul prayed, and churches were born in Asia Minor and beyond. Peter prayed, and Dorcas was raised to life (Acts 9:40).

John Wesley prayed, and revival came to England. Jonathan Edwards prayed, and revival came to America.

Who knows what amazing things the prayers of Christians today can do?

We must ask ourselves, "Why do we pray?" Do we really believe that we are speaking to almighty God? Do we really believe our voices are heard in the ear of the Lord? Do we really believe we are bowing before His throne in Heaven? Do we really believe He will answer us?

If we say yes to those questions, then why do we offer such petty petitions and go through oratorical exercises? Too often, when we start to pray, our thoughts roam. We insult God by speaking to Him with our lips while our hearts are far from Him. If we were talking to a person of prominence, would we let our thoughts wander for one moment? No. Then how dare we treat the King of kings with less respect?

The disciples who traveled with Jesus became convicted about this. They saw Jesus pray in earnest; they heard Him pray in anguish. They knew that Jesus had been in touch with God, and they wanted to have that same connection, so they said, "Lord, teach us to pray" (Luke 11:1).

He gave them a pattern prayer to follow (Matthew 6:9–13). But we find an actual prayer of Jesus in John 17.

Jesus lifted His eyes to Heaven and prayed, "Father, the hour has come. Glorify Your Son, that Your Son also may glorify You" (John 17:1). Throughout this magnificent prayer, the glory of God the Father and God the Son is exalted. Jesus had already glorified God on earth. This is a wonderful claim because He had not yet gone to the cross to finish His work; in these words He demonstrated His resolve to do what He had come to do.

"And now, O Father, glorify Me together with Yourself, with the glory which I had with You before the world was" (v. 5). We cannot pray sincerely if our aim is not to bring glory to Him.

"You have given Him authority over all flesh, that He should give eternal life. . . . that they may know You, the only true God, and Jesus Christ whom You have sent" (vv. 2–3). These verses alone demonstrate the Source of eternal life and God's everlasting authority over all people. Some may ask, "Well, if God has authority over all people, why is the world in such a mess?" The answer is because God chose, by His own authority, not to make us robots. He gave us hearts that could choose to love Him or reject Him.

Jesus offered prayer for His disciples, saying,

> "I have manifested Your name to the men whom You have given Me out of the world. . . . They have kept Your word. . . .
>
> I pray for them, . . . that they may be one as We are. . . . As You sent Me into the world, I also have sent them into the world." (vv. 6–18)

Jesus then prayed for all believers.

> "I do not pray for these [the disciples] alone, but also for those who will believe in Me . . . that they also may be one in Us. . . . And the glory which You gave Me I have given them . . . that the world may know that You have sent Me." (vv. 20–23)

This is a passage of Scripture that all Christians should commit to memory. This is where our power comes from—the Lord's prayers for His people. Even today He sits at the right hand of the Father in Heaven interceding in prayer for us (Hebrews 7:25). Through His prayers He empowers us to live for Him.

How quickly and carelessly, by contrast, we pray. Snatches of verses are hastily spoken in the morning, and then we say good-bye to God for the rest of the day until we rush through a few closing petitions at night. How little perseverance, persistence, praise, and pleading we show.

Some time ago I read about a man in Washington, DC, who had spent seventeen years securing favorable action on a claim of eighty-one thousand dollars against the government. Yet many people today will not pray seventeen minutes for the welfare of their immortal souls or for the salvation of other people.

"Pray without ceasing" (1 Thessalonians 5:17) should be the motto of every follower of Jesus Christ. Samuel prayed, "Far be it from me that I should sin against the LORD in ceasing to pray for you" (1 Samuel 12:23). Never stop praying, no matter how dark or how hopeless it may seem. Ask the Lord to help you pray that all you ask may be for the glory of the Lord Jesus Christ. This is the power of prayer.

Jesus said that His temple was a house of prayer (Matthew 21:13 NLT). God said His eternal house "shall be called a house of prayer for all nations" (Isaiah 56:7). I wonder what would happen in our churches and in our hearts if we were to begin each day reading through this marvelous prayer of our Lord from John 17.

We humans were fashioned in the beginning to live a life of prayer because prayer is fellowship with God. But sin erected a barrier between us and God. Our sin caused this great gap, but God provided His Son as our Mediator. We can know Him through reading His Word and praying to Him in His name and according to His will.

With God nothing is impossible. No task is too arduous, no problem is too difficult, and no burden is too heavy for Him. What to us are future uncertainties are fully revealed in Him. He knows what we cannot understand.

All of this should inform how we pray. Do not put your will above God's will. Do not insist on your way. Do not dictate to God. And do not expect an immediate answer, because He withholds His answers at times to grow our faith. Learn the difficult lesson of praying as the Son of God Himself prayed in Gethsemane: "Not my will, but thine, be done" (Luke 22:42 KJV).

When we pray in adversity, we may not see the full answer until we come into the peace of Heaven. When we pray in the face of danger, we may not recognize the hand of protection until we are in His care. Sadly, we are not likely to pray when we are enjoying times of prosperity, security, and freedom. Yet this is the most critical time to pray so we do not become selfish, arrogant, and captivated by the world's charms.

We have learned to harness the power of the atom and the power of technology. But we have not—nor will we ever—learn how to harness the power of sin without God's help. We have not yet learned that people can be more powerful on their knees than behind the most powerful weapon made by man.

Prayer has eternal value. We will never know the full glory of our prayers until we are in the presence of the One who answers them. Jesus is praying for us today right where He is—in Heaven eternal—just as He prayed for us while on earth. We should thank Him every day for this wonderful and precious gift.

Father, I desire that they also whom You gave
Me may be with Me *where I am*,
that they may behold My glory . . . for You loved
Me before the foundation of the world.
O righteous Father! The world has not known
You, but I have known You. . . .
And I have declared to them Your name. (John 17:24–26)

CHAPTER 19

ETERNAL REWARDS

Winning His Favor

MARK

> *You can be sure that anyone who gives up home or*
> *brothers or sisters or mother or father or children*
> *or land for me and for the good news will be*
> *rewarded. . . . And in the world to come, they will*
> *have* **eternal** *life.*

—MARK 10:29–30 CEV

A GIFT IS FREELY GIVEN; REWARDS ARE EARNED. The Bible speaks of both: gifts certainly, but also prizes and crowns. God has promised eternal rewards to those who serve Him faithfully. He has told us to store our riches where there is no corruption—in Heaven.

Receiving God's gift of salvation is what should make us want to live for Him. We cannot buy salvation, but by living a life of undivided devotion, we can "find favor and high esteem / In the sight of God" (Proverbs 3:4). The Bible says, "Without faith it is impossible to please

Him" and that "He is a rewarder of those who diligently seek Him" (Hebrews 11:6).

There were two old friends who were both dying. One was rich, the other poor. The rich man was not a Christian, but the poor man was a very strong believer in Christ. The rich man said to a visitor one day, "When I die, I shall have to leave my riches." Then he pointed to his dying friend and said, "And when he dies, he will go to his riches."

In a couple of sentences the rich man summed up a stark contrast between them. The man who possessed everything on earth in reality had nothing. The man with nothing on earth in reality had everything.

This is a vivid illustration of what Jesus said to His disciples:

> "Do not lay up for yourselves treasures on earth, where moth and rust destroy . . . but lay up for yourselves treasures in heaven. . . . For where your treasure is, there your heart will be also." (Matthew 6:19–21)

Does that mean that we must renounce everything we own? No—not unless God clearly commands us to do so. But it does mean we commit everything we have—including our lives—to Christ. We are to put our love for Him above everything else.

Many years ago, back in the 1880s, the famous preacher Dwight L. Moody felt God leading him to hold an evangelistic meeting at Cambridge University. Many said it was a futile task. He went anyway, and people sneered at his effort. Halfway through the series of meetings, though, things turned around and many responded to the invitation. Hundreds more surrendered their lives in service to God. Moody was storing up treasures in Heaven.

Out of this mission came the famous Cambridge Seven, seven young men who joined Hudson Taylor's China Inland Mission. One of them was C. T. Studd, the son of a wealthy man and captain of the prestigious Cambridge University cricket team, who sensed God's call to missionary work in China.

At the age of twenty-five, the young man inherited a fortune from his father's estate. He promptly gave it all away to Christian work, keeping nothing for himself—not even for his own work in Asia. Then at the age of fifty and in poor health after years in China and India, he felt God's call to take the Gospel to Africa. After his first visit he wrote:

> Last June at the mouth of the Congo there awaited a thousand prospectors, traders, merchants and gold seekers, waiting to rush into these regions as soon as the government opened the door to them, for rumor declared that there is an abundance of gold. If such men hear so loudly the call of gold and obey it, can it be that the ears of Christ's soldiers are deaf to the call of God, and the cries of the dying souls of men? Are gamblers for gold so many, and risk takers so few for God?[1]

Studd is just one of multitudes of people who have surrendered their lives to Christ and walked away from lucrative businesses, successful jobs, and easygoing lifestyles to serve Him in difficult places.

William Borden, heir to the Borden family fortune, was another young man burdened for lost souls in Asia. A friend wrote to Bill that he was throwing his life away to be a missionary. But Borden wrote in his Bible, "No reserves." Upon graduating from Yale in 1909, he turned down many lucrative job offers and wrote in his Bible, "No retreats." When he finished his graduate work at Princeton, he sailed to Egypt to study Arabic in hopes of working with Muslims. While there he contracted spinal meningitis. Within a month twenty-five-year-old Borden was dead. Many speculated that his death was a waste. In time it was discovered that Borden had written two more words in his Bible beneath his other entries: "No reserves. No retreats. No regrets."[2]

Borden had stored up treasure in Heaven that far exceeded the vast wealth he had given away on earth. Time revealed that his testimony had caused many others to serve God with their lives. Christ Himself "will reward each according to his works" (Matthew 16:27).

There is a group of men in Scripture who also walked away from their life's work to follow Christ; many of them were fishermen from Galilee. The Gospels give us a wonderful glimpse into a conversation between Jesus and His disciples. Peter said, "See, we have left all and followed You" (Mark 10:28).

Jesus knows the motives, thoughts, and intents of the heart. "*I am* He who searches the minds and hearts. And I will give to each one of you according to your works" (Revelation 2:23). So He understood exactly why Peter was making this point. Jesus answered him with reassurance:

> "There is no one who has left house or brothers or sisters or father or mother or wife or children or lands, for My sake and the gospel's, who shall not receive a hundredfold now in this time . . . and in the age to come, eternal life." (vv. 29–30)

He was telling Peter—and us—that He would provide and that all the sacrifice would be worth it.

While much is said about Christian workers who are publicly visible, not much is said anymore about the quiet works of God's servants. We will have to get to Heaven before we will fully realize the army of prayer warriors that made others' work possible. Just as the church is the body of Christ, the work is never accomplished by the act of just one, unless it is Christ's alone. "For we are God's fellow workers; you are God's field, you are God's building" (1 Corinthians 3:9).

This is what Paul explained to the church at Corinth when a controversy stirred up about who should get credit for works done in Jesus' name. Some had come to know Christ by the works of Paul, Apollos, and others preaching the Gospel. Paul wrote to them that the Lord had given responsibilities to each one, but that the results belonged to Him (vv. 5–7).

In our crusades over the years, we have watched the body of Christ operating in various ways—churches recruiting volunteers to help with parking, ushering, counseling, giving financially, and, most important, praying for the lost. All of these who have quietly and faithfully worked behind the scenes will be rewarded by the Lord Himself someday.

There are those who minister to others by their presence in hospital waiting rooms and at funeral homes, when family and friends are in need and mourning loss. This used to be a wonderful ministry outreach but is less popular today. The Lord is watching those who are faithful in giving themselves and their time to bring comfort to those who need it. I think of my own mother, who was an avid letter writer, encouraging others with a word from Scripture. This, too, is service to God.

Then there are those who point people to the Savior by how they live, day in and day out. Parents who are faithful to each other and to their children, living examples who speak of Christ's virtues, instilling Christian character into the fabric of life so that when they are with others, no one can find fault in how they live. Christ will reward them.

> In all things showing yourself to be a pattern of good works; in doctrine showing integrity, reverence, incorruptibility, sound speech that cannot be condemned, that one who is an opponent may be ashamed, having nothing evil to say of you. (Titus 2:7–8)

There are young people, too, who stand strong among their peers without compromise. They may be laughed at or worse because they won't participate in dishonorable behavior. This pleases the Lord, and He will reward them because they honored him and exhibited a steadfast witness. "Therefore, my beloved brethren, be steadfast, immovable, always abounding in the work of the Lord, knowing that your labor is not in vain in the Lord" (1 Corinthians 15:58). Living obediently for the Lord is service to Him.

Most important, though, is that God tells us to store up the right kind of riches in our lives. We often think of riches in a monetary or materialistic way, but God speaks of riches that don't fade away. He will deposit His riches in our hearts, creating an inward righteousness that produces the marks of a true believer in Christ (Ephesians 2:6–8).

When we possess the richness of salvation, our storehouse here will be full to overflowing with the fruit of the Spirit, unspeakable joy, peace that passes all understanding, wisdom, strength, and the love of Christ.

Someone has said that these are the beautiful jewels in heavenly crowns because they are the attributes of Christ.

In Heaven there will be many believers who never received any acknowledgment while on earth, yet they faithfully prayed and humbly served Christ. I believe their crowns may sparkle with more jewels than the philanthropist who endowed the church and whose name is engraved on the plaque in the narthex. Paul warned the wealthy not to be haughty, not to seek men's approval, but God's (Galatians 1:10).

Moses gave up all earthly glory and possessions to identify with God's people. He was the adopted child of an Egyptian princess, but he gave up the kingdom and crown of Egypt to be a child of God. He was educated in the finest schools, but he gave up the prestige to learn the wisdom of God. Moses gave up the royal scepter to be rich in God's law. The prophet was known as a shepherd, a leader, a deliverer, a lawgiver, and a judge. But Moses said, "O my Lord, I am . . . Your servant" (Exodus 4:10); and when he died, God spoke of him as, "Moses My servant" (Joshua 1:2).

When you reach Heaven, there will be no opportunity to brag of your exploits, your ambitions, or the joys of your pleasure; but you will have eternity to rejoice in how you lived your life for Jesus because of His grace in you.

It may take a lifetime to accumulate wealth, but it can vanish in the blink of an eye. While the Bible teaches us to store up treasures in Heaven, the greatest treasure is in knowing that we will be rewarded by His very presence—forevermore.

Whatever you do, do it heartily, as to the Lord and not to men,
knowing that from the Lord you will receive
the reward of the inheritance;
for you serve the Lord Christ. (Colossians 3:23–24)

CHAPTER 20

THE SEARCH FOR ETERNAL LIFE

Running to Him, Then Walking Away

LUKE

Teacher, what shall I do to inherit **eternal** *life?*

—LUKE 10:25

WALKING ACROSS A UNIVERSITY CAMPUS TO GIVE AN ADDRESS SOME YEARS AGO, A STUDENT STOPPED ME AND SAID, "MR. GRAHAM, WE HEAR A LOT ABOUT THE VALUE OF RELIGION, BUT NOBODY TELLS US HOW TO FIND CHRIST." Since then, I have tried to explain simply and plainly how to find Jesus and inherit what He promised—eternal life.

We may believe that young people do not think deeply about life, but perhaps that is because we are not listening. The reality is that people of all ages sense that there is something more than just the here and now. They are right; God has set eternity in the human heart (Ecclesiastes 3:11 NASB).

When 1970s television talk-show host Dick Cavett was asked if there was life after death, he responded that he did not have the answer. There are various accounts in Scripture of people asking this question about life beyond the grave. The answer leads to Christ, but many ignore it because they do not want the truth.

This was the case with a young man who had everything: wealth, youth, and powerful authority. But he was not satisfied; anxiously he sought eternal life. Money could not buy it. Youth could not guarantee it. And power could not gain it. So in his search he determined his goodness could earn it.

The Bible says that he went to Jesus; an aristocrat fell at the feet of a penniless prophet. There's no doubt that this young man sought Jesus at the right time—with urgency, he ran to Him. He came in the right way—humbly, he knelt before Jesus. He asked the right Person the right question: "Good Teacher, what good thing shall I do that I may have eternal life?" (Matthew 19:16).

Jesus answered directly, telling him to keep the commandments and he would obtain eternal life. The rich young ruler asked, "Which ones?" (v. 18). He wouldn't have asked had he kept them all. Jesus knew. He was not only listening; He was looking into his heart.

Then the young man asked, "What do I still lack?" (v. 20). He was focused on his "goodness" instead of his sinfulness; he lacked repentance; he wanted to do a "good thing" to inherit eternal life. So Jesus put him to the test, revealing the young man's selfish heart.

> Then Jesus, looking at him, loved him, and said to him, "One thing you lack: Go your way, sell whatever you have and give to the poor, and you will have treasure in heaven; and come, take up the cross, and follow Me.
>
> But [the young man] was sad at this word, and went away sorrowful, for he had great possessions. (Mark 10:21–22)

This man stood before Jesus having riches, rank, and religion, but he did not see himself as a sinner. He couldn't fathom the reality that "all have sinned and fall short of the glory of God" (Romans 3:23). By his own admission, he did not fit into this category. Though he had humbled himself by kneeling at Jesus' feet, his heart did not bow. He wanted the *forever* life, not the *faithful* life. Jesus promised him the very thing he said he wanted most—eternal life—but would not accept at the expense of his treasures. He wanted both—his way.

The young man walked away disappointed with his encounter with Jesus. Perhaps he was expecting Jesus to give him a weekend assignment to feed the poor or a command to give money to a widow's home. But to give up what was dearest to him was out of the question.

Jesus was not against the man keeping his money. Jesus was against money keeping the man from following Him. This young man trusted more in his riches than in Jesus' word and therefore rejected the Answer.

A lawyer also came to Jesus with the same question: "Teacher, what shall I do to inherit eternal life?" (Luke 10:25). Jesus answered him with a question: "What is written in the law?" (v. 26).

The man replied, "'You shall love the LORD your God with all your heart . . . soul . . . strength, and . . . mind,' and 'your neighbor as yourself'" (v. 27). Jesus said, "You have answered rightly; do this and you will live" (v. 28).

But the man really was not interested in the truth; he was trying to trick Jesus and asked, "And who is my neighbor?" (v. 29).

The lawyer put the emphasis on the neighbor while Jesus had emphasized loving the Lord foremost. This reflects many hearts today. Our tendency is to put the greater emphasis on our neighbor while ignoring God. We are commanded to "do unto others," but our first responsibility is to obey Him, for it is only through His power that we can reach out to actually help others. Jesus demonstrated this by telling a story.

A certain man went down from Jerusalem to Jericho, and fell among thieves, who stripped him of his clothing, wounded him, and departed, leaving him half dead. [Then] a certain priest came down that road. And when he saw him, he passed by on the other side. Likewise a Levite . . . came and looked, and passed by on the other side. But a certain Samaritan, as he journeyed, came where he was. And when he saw him, he had compassion. (vv. 30–33)

Jericho was a thriving border city teeming with international travelers and bandits, a place filled with thieves, deceivers, and passers-by. It was also a city filled with religious teachers. Here we see two of the three travelers deliberately pass by "on the other side."

The priest, who represents religion in all its forms, was the first to close his eyes to the one in need. Paul would later write to Timothy of those "having a form of godliness but denying its power" (2 Timothy 3:5). Religion saves no one. Jesus said, "You . . . justify yourselves before men, but God knows your hearts. For what is highly esteemed among men is an abomination in the sight of God" (Luke 16:15).

The Levite, who represents the law, also looked at the wounded man but ignored his peril. He, too, walked away.

There are people who say they can be saved by doing the best they can or by keeping the law. Others believe they will go to Heaven based on their good deeds. Some just say they are not sure. You don't have to be unsure. The Bible is absolutely clear on what is needed. John said, "These things I have written to you who believe in the name of the Son of God, that you may know that you have eternal life, and that you may continue to believe in the name of the Son of God" (1 John 5:13).

How? The Bible tells us that too: "But when the kindness and the love of God our Savior toward man appeared, not by works of righteousness which we have done, but according to His mercy He saved us. . . . that . . . we should become heirs according to the hope of eternal life" (Titus 3:4–7).

The priest and the Levite on that road to Jericho were unwilling to help, so the wounded man was left to die. I remember being in London years ago and reading about a woman who died at the age of 102. She had made a nightly entry in her diary: "No one called today. No one loves me." She died alone.

This is what could have happened to the wounded man—if a certain Samaritan hadn't come along. The Samaritan was despised by both Jews and Gentiles, but when he saw the dying man, he was filled with compassion. He bent down and bandaged the man's wounds, pouring on oil and wine, and then set him on his own animal, brought him to an inn, took care of him, saved his life, and left money to sustain him until he could travel.

Here was a man who gave his resources and his time for another. He even used his own "ambulance" to transport the wounded man, taking him to what was probably the first Samaritan Hospital.

Luke is the only biblical writer to record this remarkable story. Because he was a physician, Luke emphasized how the Samaritan cared for the man's wounds. Pouring on oil speaks of the Holy Spirit and reminds us that Jesus was anointed with oil before His own death. Wine—the most potent of ancient antiseptics—speaks of the blood of Christ, which cleanses from sin.

What a picture this is of the Savior who came to this dying world— the land of the walking dead—with the infectious disease of sin. He didn't just pass by. Christ stooped down in compassion and carried our sins to the cross. He paid the price to redeem us and will lift us up to eternal life with Him someday.

The prophet Isaiah wrote of the Savior:

> He has sent Me to heal the brokenhearted,
> To proclaim liberty to the captives . . .
> To give them beauty for ashes,
> The oil of joy for mourning,
> The garment of praise for the spirit of heaviness . . .
> That He may be glorified. (Isaiah 61:1–3)

What a wonderful opportunity we have to help others find the Savior and encourage them in living for the Lord. Christ gave His all for us as an example of how we should live.

One day at Stanford University, a student of a non-Christian faith came to me and said that he was convinced Jesus is the Son of God but that he couldn't confess Him publicly because in his home country the social cost would be too great.

I told him what the Bible says: "Whoever confesses Me before men, him I will also confess before My Father who is in heaven. But whoever denies Me before men, him I will also deny before My Father who is in heaven" (Matthew 10:32–33).

Like the rich young ruler, that student went away sad. He had counted the cost and was not willing to pay it. He wasn't ready to put Christ first.

When ambassadors serve their countries, they cannot do so effectively if they are ashamed of whom they represent, even more so if one claims to serve the King of kings.

After Jesus ascended to Heaven, the apostles stood before their peers, their families, and their communities and governments unashamed of the Lord Jesus Christ. They blazed a trail for all who would come after them.

Jesus did not come into this world to start a new religion; He came to give life to those who were dead in trespasses and sin. "For the wages of sin is death, but the gift of God is eternal life in Christ Jesus our Lord" (Romans 6:23).

While preaching my last crusade in New York in 2005, I told about a young man who wrote, "All of my life I built up to this one moment of decision—when I ran out of myself and let God take over." How about you? If you are disappointed with your encounter with Jesus Christ, it is because you have not "run out of yourself." End your search today for this eternal gift. Lay hold of it through repentance. Then let God take over and fill you with His abundant grace.

He who loves his life will lose it, and he who
hates his life in this world will keep it
for eternal life. If anyone serves Me, let him follow Me;
and *where I am*, there My servant will be also.
If anyone serves Me, him My Father will honor. (John 12:25–26)

CHAPTER 21

HOME ETERNAL— WHERE I AM

Life Everlasting

JOHN

For God so loved the world that He gave His only begotten Son, that whoever believes in Him should not perish but have **everlasting** *life. . . .*
That **where I am***, there you may be also.*

—JOHN 3:16; 14:3

"I DON'T THINK I WOULD BE AFRAID TO DIE IF I KNEW WHAT TO EXPECT AFTER DEATH," SAID A YOUNG MAN WITH AN INCURABLE DISEASE. Evidently he had not heard of what God "has prepared for those who love Him" (1 Corinthians 2:9).

This young man had within him the fear of death. By nature, we fear the unknown. But the Bible says that the grave is not the end for anyone but rather the beginning of eternity:

Transgressors and sinners . . .
Who forsake the LORD shall be consumed. . . .
Both will burn together,
And no one shall quench them. (Isaiah 1:28, 31)

This is not God's will but a consequence of human choice.

The child of God has no need to fear death. Why? God has not left us with the spirit of hopelessness, for He is "the God of hope" (Romans 15:13). Death, for the Christian, is overcome by the reality of hope—Heaven.

We see this assurance in John, the great *"Where I am"* book of the Bible. Jesus had told His disciples He was going away; He was preparing them for His death. But they could not fathom what He was telling them. They had walked with Him and fellowshiped together. He was their Teacher and Friend; they were His students and His companions.

Peter said to Him, "Lord, where are You going?"
Jesus answered him, *"Where I am* going you cannot follow Me now." (John 13:36)

Then Jesus spoke some of the most treasured words in Scripture:

"Let not your heart be troubled; you believe in God, believe also in Me. In My Father's house are many mansions; if it were not so, I would have told you. I go to prepare a place for you. . . . I will come again and receive you to Myself; that *where I am*, there you may be also. And where I go you know, and the way you know." (14:1–4)

This was a revelation to the disciples. It was as if Jesus had said to them, "We have no lasting home on earth, but My Father's house is a home where we will be together forever." This is a picture painted with words—for He is the Word. A heavenly home is described in the Greek as a "mansion." It doesn't mean an imposing house but rather a permanent dwelling—an eternal abode. Jesus told this little band of men the way to reach this wonderful place: "I am the way, the truth, and the life. No one comes to the Father except through Me" (v. 6).

As humans we place a great deal of value on our homes. Amid all the changes that will come, when we no longer have an earthly home, we have a promise—we will be with Him forever.

Heaven seems a mystery to many people. They wonder if Heaven is above the lofty clouds, or if Heaven will come down to earth. When I am asked, "Where is Heaven?" I simply answer: Heaven is where Jesus is. He told His disciples, "I go to prepare a place for you . . . that *where I am*, there you may be also!" So when my earthly life has ended and you wonder where I've gone, this will be the answer: I will be with Jesus—that's *where I am*.

What about you? Do you know where you will be when you step into eternity? The ultimate destination is not found in a slick vacation package. The ultimate destination is Heaven—found in Jesus Christ. Nothing can transcend this wonderful place. Jesus said, "If anyone loves Me, he will keep My word; and My Father will love him, and We will come to him and make Our home with him" (v. 23).

Nicodemus was a Pharisee who had heard of Jesus and was interested in what He had to say, so he went looking for Him. We don't know where he found Jesus, for He had no earthly home. "Foxes have holes," He said, "and birds of the air have nests, but the Son of Man has nowhere to lay His head" (Matthew 8:20). But the Bible says that if we seek Him, He may be found (Isaiah 55:6, Matthew 7:7). And, sure enough, Nicodemus found Jesus in the dark of night.

"Rabbi," he said, "we know that You are a teacher come from God; for no one can do these signs that You do unless God is with him" (John 3:2).

Jesus changed the conversation from the miracles of which Nicodemus inquired to the miracle of a new life in Christ and said,

> "Unless one is born again, he cannot see the kingdom of God. . . . That which is born of the flesh is flesh, and that which is born of the Spirit is spirit. Do not marvel that I said to you, 'You must be born again.'" (vv. 3, 6–7)

Nicodemus' reaction was filled with doubt and unbelief, and he exclaimed, "How can these things be?" (v. 9).

Jesus answered this leading Pharisee with another question. "Are you the teacher of Israel, and do not know these things?" (v. 10).

Nicodemus was stunned. If Christ had said this to Zacchaeus or the woman at the well, it might make sense, but Jesus spoke to a professor of theology. And He was saying, "It isn't enough, Nicodemus. You must be born again."

This term *born again* has fascinated people for centuries. It simply means "born from above"— born into the family of God. We are all God's creation, but we are not all God's children. Those who are born only once (physical birth) will experience physical and spiritual death, what the Bible calls the second death. But those who are born twice (physically and spiritually) will die only a physical death because they will be resurrected to life eternal. This is why Jesus came.

Nicodemus could only see human life; Jesus was speaking of spiritual life. What Nicodemus needed was a new heart. Surely he would have read the Scripture, "I will give you a new heart and put a new spirit within you" (Ezekiel 36:26). No matter how hard Nicodemus worked to live right, he fell short of being born again.

This was a lot for Nicodemus to take in. Imagine what must have been going through his mind when he heard Jesus say,

"For God so loved the world that He gave His only begotten Son, that whoever believes in Him should not perish but have everlasting life. For God did not send His Son into the world to condemn the world, but that the world through Him might be saved." (John 3:16–17)

The Bible does not record what happened after their meeting; and if the book of John ended there, we might not know what became of Nicodemus. But John 7 tells of a debate that later arose among the Jewish leaders about Jesus, for He had told them also that He was going away, and *"where I am* you cannot come" (vv. 33–34). Jesus knew the chief priests were planning to seize Him, but He spoke of returning to His heavenly home. Then the Pharisees asked one another if any of them believed Jesus, and Scripture says that Nicodemus spoke up for Him (vv. 47–50). Jesus' words had illuminated Nicodemus' darkened heart.

We don't see Nicodemus again until he appears after Christ's death on the cross, bringing a mixture of spices to use in preparing Jesus' body for burial (19:39). Most of Christ's followers had fled, but here we see Nicodemus caring for Him. It seems that even in death's shadow, Nicodemus had eternity on his mind.

But as we've seen, many people never think of eternity. As a Christian and a preacher of the Gospel, I am always grieved to have to interrupt a marvelous picture, such as eternal life in Heaven, to talk about another eternal place that Jesus calls Hell. It has no similarities to what is typically called home, nor is Hell a resting place, a holding place, or a graveyard. Hell is a burning inferno.

More than the description, I want to point out the greatest darkness of Hell—it is a place *where Jesus is not.* Jesus said, "I am going away. You will search for me but will die in your sin. You cannot come *where I am going*" (8:21 NLT). This is the great anguishing nightmare—to be eternally separated from the Son of God. It is unimaginable. For this reason alone, to be in Hell is the most terrible of all judgments.

There are some people who actually believe that if they end up in Hell, they'll get used to it. After all, they say, the devil has provided a great deal of pleasure for them while on earth, so how bad can it be?

Let me tell you; the devil is not in charge of Hell, nor is it his headquarters. Satan is the "prince of this world" (16:11 KJV) and has taken up residence in many hearts. But He knows what the end is for him. He made his choice long ago and wants to take a world of people with him to Hell, where he will serve out his eternal sentence.

The Bible says that the everlasting fire was created for the devil and his angels (Matthew 25:41). Jesus said, "I have the keys of Hades and of Death" (Revelation 1:18). The devil does not own Hell. It is not his home—it is his judgment.

161

A mother and son once lived in a miserable attic. Years before, she had married against her parents' wishes and had gone with her husband to live in a strange land. But her husband soon died, and she managed with great difficulty to secure the bare necessities. The boy's happiest times were when his mother told of her father's house in the old country, a place with grassy lawns, enormous trees, wide porches, and delicious meals. The child longed to live there.

One day the postman knocked at the door with a letter. The woman recognized her father's handwriting and with trembling fingers opened the envelope that held a check and a slip of paper with two words: "Come home."

A similar experience will come to all who know Christ. Someday you will receive this brief message: "The Father says come home."

Those who know Christ are not afraid to die. Death is not the grim reaper. Death to the Christian is "going home." No one who has died in the Lord would ever want to come back to this life. To depart and be with Christ, Paul said, "is far better" (Philippians 1:23). The Bible says that we are strangers and pilgrims on earth seeking a homeland, a place prepared for us by God (Hebrews 11:16) where the Lord will receive us into "an everlasting home" (Luke 16:9). I have never known a man or woman to receive Christ and ever regret it.

Perhaps you have never bent your will to God's will and been born again. You can do that now, for He desires that all be saved (1 Timothy 2:4). Right now you can make your decision for Christ and start on the road that leads to a *heavenly* home.

Jesus said in essence, "You can be *where I am*, or you can be *where I am not*." I pray you settle life's most important question: Where will you spend eternity?

My witness is true, for I know where I came
from and *where I am* going. (John 8:14)

CHAPTER 22

ETERNAL WORKS OF GOD

Idols Are Idle—God Is at Work

ACTS

Known to God from **eternity** *are all His works.*

—ACTS 15:18

WAITING FOR HIS FRIENDS, PAUL TOOK A WALK THROUGH THE
STREETS OF ATHENS, THE CITY OF GREEK INTELLECTS LIKE
SOCRATES, ARISTOTLE, AND PLATO. The Grecians excelled in education; their language skills were masterful. But Paul's spirit was troubled
because the city had been "given over to idols" (Acts 17:16).

As always, Paul went to the synagogues and reasoned with the Jews,
and also the Gentiles, concerning Jesus and the resurrection. Daily in the
marketplace he felt the urge to preach to those milling about. Epicurean
and Stoic philosophers scoffed, saying, "What does this babbler want to
say?" and "He seems to be a proclaimer of foreign gods" (v. 18).

Paul was given a forceful escort to the Areopagus, named for the
Roman god of war, and also known as Mars Hill. This was the court of

law, where people gave speeches and debated world problems. While on the way, the men said to him, "May we know what this new doctrine is of which you speak? For you are bringing up some strange things to our ears. . . . We want to know what these things mean" (vv. 19–20).

Why did they want to hear from Paul? He stood out from the crowd. He didn't apologize for his message; he proclaimed it with boldness. Athenians were always seeking "some new thing" (v. 21), so as Paul moved toward Mars Hill, he found the topic for his message.

Standing in the midst of the crowd, he said,

"Men of Athens, I perceive that in all things you are very religious; for as I was passing through and considering the objects of your worship, I even found an altar with this inscription:

TO THE UNKNOWN GOD.

Therefore, the One whom you worship without knowing, Him I proclaim to you." (vv. 22–23)

Paul had observed their customs; their moral corruption was revealed by the hundreds of idols illuminated by the sun. This pagan society had a niche for every god in the world. They worshiped the constellations and the physical body, and they indulged every obsession that gave them pleasure. And in case they missed one, they had even erected a statue to represent the unknown god.

Standing before the Parthenon, which housed the city's immense symbols of progress, Paul challenged the great statue of Athena, made of gold and ivory, which represented the goddess of nature. Then, in great power, this Gospel preacher proceeded to tell them about the One who had created the world and everything in it. Let's listen to Paul, because the Lord spoke through him to the pagan heart.

"God, who made the world and everything in it . . . does not dwell in temples made with hands. Nor is He worshiped with men's hands, as though He needed anything, since He gives to all life, breath, and all things. And He has made from one blood every nation of men to dwell on all the face of the earth, and has determined their pre-appointed times and the boundaries of their dwellings, so that they should seek the Lord, in the hope that they might [reach] for Him and find Him, though He is not far from each one of us." (vv. 24–27)

In a few sentences Paul dismantled the false power of the gods to whom the Athenians looked upon and bowed down. He proclaimed the true God who gives meaning to life, the One who looks down from Heaven into stony human hearts. This message was unlike anything they had ever heard. He continued to point to their own objects made of stone as he spoke:

"Some of your own poets have said, 'For we are also His offspring.' Therefore, since we are the offspring of God, we ought not to think that the Divine Nature is like gold or silver or stone, something shaped by art and man's devising. Truly, these times of ignorance God overlooked, but now commands all men everywhere to repent, because He has appointed a day on which He will judge the world in righteousness by the Man whom He has ordained. He has given assurance of this to all by raising Him from the dead." (vv. 28–31)

My, what a sermon! Paul got right to the heart of the matter—the resurrection of the One who will bring eternal life to their hardened hearts through repentance. This was something new. The Athenians hadn't stopped to consider their dark side. They'd been too busy making gods like themselves.

I would imagine there were gasps from the assembly when Paul found a point of connection. He used the words of their own poets to bring them to a point of agreement, but still, Paul's message divided the city.

When some heard about the resurrection from the dead, they mocked him; others wanted to hear more. When Paul walked away, some men joined him and believed. I can assure you Paul's heart was overjoyed because God had been faithful in giving him the words, and he had been faithful in proclaiming the message. This is what the Lord calls us to do. The results belong to Him.

In Paul's experience that day, we see three typical responses to the Gospel: derision, delay, and decision. I have seen people at our crusades laugh and scoff at the preaching of God's Word. I have seen people troubled by the truth but who end up walking away. And then I have stood and watched as people got up out of their seats and responded to the invitation in a spirit of repentance.

Let's look at these three groups. Those responding with *derision* (disbelief) refuse to consider what Christ has done for them. And if the truth were known, most simply do not want to give up their own ways—sinful pleasure and false religion—to receive salvation. That's sad, but even sadder are those who refuse to repent for fear of ridicule by their friends. Salvation will win you no popularity contest on earth, but it will win eternal life.

You cannot reform your way to heaven, rationalize your way to heaven, or moralize your way to heaven. You cannot work your way there. Only one choice will save your soul: repent of sin and receive Christ as your Lord and Savior. Then you must lay down your ego, your selfishness, and your pride and take up the cross of Christ. He will help you do this.

Some believe that carrying your cross means to hang one around your neck, but that will not cleanse your soul. The cross of Christ—for you—may be persecution in various forms. You may lose jobs or be deserted by family and friends. Many today are losing their lives for the name of Christ—and Heaven welcomes them.

For those who *delay*, they think they have all the time in the world. This is dangerous, because they may never again have the same opportunity. When I was in Sydney, Australia, years ago preaching this message, I was given a handwritten note that said, "The most dangerous day in life is when you find out how easy it is to talk about tomorrow."

Those who come to *decision* are not choosing if they will enter eternity. They are rather choosing to enter life or to enter death. Why is something that seems so easy so difficult? It's because the majority of people refuse to believe they are sinners.

All humanity starts out on level ground—all are sinners. But by God's grace, He forgives and redeems. It is human nature to seek something to believe in. Those who reject Christ put their faith in something, even if just themselves.

The city of Athens in Paul's day was not much different from today's carnal culture, filled with idol worshipers. Do what Paul did: take a walk through your home and neighborhood. Observe what catches your attention.

We are an obsessed society accumulating material possessions, building our bodies to impress others, worshiping money and devising ways to get more, flaunting power and position to lord over others, and educating while exchanging truths for lies. Our society is persuaded by sex-driven minds, where advertisers appeal to lustful eyes to sell even motor oil and cereal. Religious services now focus on good deeds as an acceptable replacement for living in obedience to Christ. Our culture is saturated with the worship of sports rather than worship of the Savior. We are educating the mind and neglecting the soul.

The Bible says, "For men will be lovers of themselves . . . lovers of pleasure rather than lovers of God, having a form of godliness but denying its power. And from such people turn away!" (2 Timothy 3:2–5).

We are busy humanizing God and deifying man. Our idols are not statues made of gold and marble; our idols come from entertainment, technology, and fashion industries, with "self" centered in the midst. Mankind works awfully hard to be comfortable in sin.

Some years ago a blockbuster movie came out of Hollywood titled *Children of a Lesser God*. This title is a good description of what people have always done: wanting to worship someone like themselves. Anything other than God is less than His intentions for the human race, and He is not winking.

In this marvelous Bible passage, we see Paul setting the record straight, leaving his audience with some food for thought as they consider the eternal works of the Lord. Whether the hearers believed or not, they went away persuaded, perplexed, or indifferent.

Paul was not deterred by those who rejected his message. When his fellow Jews refused to listen, he wrote, "Since you reject it, and judge yourselves unworthy of everlasting life, behold, we turn to the Gentiles" (Acts 13:46). This very message turned the world of that day upside down (17:6). Paul reminded his Gentile listeners that while they thought God was far from them, He, in fact, was not far away at all and could be found. His works were from eternity past, and His works will be fully revealed in eternity to come.

This message for the people of the ancient world is for us today, and it will be *the* message in the end times. Paul continually stressed that he was first a sinner saved by grace. Scripture tells us that he was a missionary and church planter, an evangelist and a servant of the living God, who was called to preach the Gospel primarily to the Gentile world. And we see just how effectively he did so through the Spirit's guidance.

Do we stand out from the crowd because of the message we proclaim? The Bible says, "Labor for [what] . . . endures to everlasting life. . . . This is the work of God, that you believe in Him whom He sent" (John 6:27-29). Do people see something in us that speaks of God's work in the hearts of men and women?

As we marvel at the "acts of the apostles," we, too, can proclaim the boldness of Christ's message by living life in a way that causes others to say, "We want to hear more about what you believe." This is our mission—to speak of the eternal works of Jesus Christ and be at work when He comes again.

The works of His hands. . . .
They stand fast forever and ever. (Psalm 111:7-8)

CHAPTER 23

PRAISE ETERNAL

Suffering or Singing

ROMANS

*[Christ] is God, the one who rules over everything
and is worthy of **eternal** praise!*

—ROMANS 9:5 NLT

JESUS CHRIST WILL BE PRAISED ETERNALLY. When we look back over the years at what God has done through our crusade ministry, we give Him praise for the privilege of preaching His Gospel. We give Him praise for answering the prayers of His people. We praise Him for souls won to the kingdom. But even more than this is our praise for Jesus Christ Himself and His great love that never fails.

Scripture speaks of praising the Lord continually and forever, in the past, present, and future. Praise should be on our lips and in our hearts. It should be demonstrated in our lives because this will be the grandeur of Heaven—praising Him eternally. It would serve us well to study passages that lift Him high.

The patriarchs praised the Lord throughout the generations. The prophets praised Him for deliverance. The apostles praised Christ in all of His glory, and the people praised the Messiah who came and is coming again. The praise did not flow only in times of victory, but also in times of imprisonment, in times of despair, and in the face of death.

One of the most compelling passages about praise, however, is when Jesus Himself praised His Father in Heaven for revealing the truth to the people whose ears and hearts had been opened to the Gospel. He had been preaching this message to Jewish leaders, but they rejected His message and sought to kill Him. He rebuked them for scoffing at those who had received His Word with gladness. Then He prayed, "I praise You, Father, Lord of heaven and earth, that You have hidden these things from the wise and intelligent and have revealed them to infants" (Matthew 11:25 NASB).

Long after the resurrection, Peter wrote to believers who had been persecuted for their faith. He encouraged them to keep their hearts on Christ and told them about the inheritance they would receive in Heaven. "So when your faith remains strong through many trials, it will bring you much praise and glory and honor on the day when Jesus Christ is revealed to the whole world" (1 Peter 1:7 NLT).

The Bible urges the body of Christ—the church—to encourage one another in praise of the Savior. Today while the Lord tarries, persecution of God's faithful may become widespread. We must keep in mind that while it is difficult, He will be with us, and the trials we endure for His sake will strengthen us in faith and open doors so that we can speak boldly for Him.

> If any man speak, let him speak as the oracles of God; if any man minister, let him do it as of the ability which God giveth: that God in all things may be glorified through Jesus Christ, to whom be praise and dominion for ever and ever. (4:11 KJV)

"Praise and worship" has become a cliché in many Christian circles. Do we really stop long enough to consider what it means and how it affects our daily lives? Praising the Lord is not something we are called to do on Sunday morning. It is a way of life—praising God no matter what we do or where we are. As believers we are to function by the power of God, who does all things well.

It is relatively easy to go to church and sing for an hour, but it is another matter entirely to live day in and day out praising the Lord with our obedience. When we are discouraged, "praise Him" (Psalm 42:5). Praise to God is the antidote for every trouble. When we praise Him, we are worshiping Him by keeping our eyes on Him.

In the middle of the Old Testament we find the hymnbook that God inspired and that Jesus sang from in the Upper Room the night before His death (Matthew 26:30). The 150 psalms speak of praise well over 150 times. Our imagination cannot begin to fathom what it must have been like to see Jesus sitting with the disciples, singing hymns of praise, knowing that the very next day He would die for the sins of the world. Many theologians believe that Jesus would have led the disciples in the Hallel psalms (praise hymns), which appear in various chapters of the book of Psalms:

> In You, O Lord, I put my trust. . . .
> You are my rock and my fortress . . .
> Lead me and guide me.
> Pull me out of the net which they have secretly laid
>   for me,
> For You are my strength.
> Into Your hand I commit my spirit;
> You have redeemed me, O Lord God of truth.
>   (31:1, 3–5)

> The pains of death surrounded me,
> And the pangs of Sheol laid hold of me;
> I found trouble and sorrow.
> Then I called upon the name of the Lord;

"O Lord, I implore You, deliver my soul!"
I will take up the cup of salvation,
And call upon the name of the Lord. (116:3–4, 13)

I will praise You,
For You have answered me. . . .

The stone which the builders rejected
Has become the chief cornerstone.
This was the Lord's doing. (118:21–23)

Consider these few examples and then remember what the Lord said from the cross a few hours later: "Father, 'into Your hands I commit My spirit'" (Luke 23:46).

If our Lord could sing praise in the face of His gruesome death, should we not be mindful always to think, speak, sing, and praise Him continually? We should; we will spend eternity praising Him. Do not forsake the preparation of the heart when praising the Lord of Heaven, for He is worthy of genuine praise, not just lip service.

How should we praise? The psalmist tells us to praise Him with an upright heart (Psalm 32:11), to lift up our heads in praise (27:6), to use our tongues to praise His righteousness (35:28), to praise Him in conversation (50:23), to praise Him when we need to wait patiently (52:9), and to pray continually with praise (72:15).

Scripture tells us to direct our praise upward, not inward. Paul in particular tells us that a changed heart seeks praise from God, not from people (Romans 2:29). We all need to be reminded of this important truth: if we are seeking approval and praise from others, we do not have our minds on Christ and His glory.

In God we boast all day long,
And praise Your name forever. (Psalm 44:8)

In good times and troubled times, praise the Lord for His promise that He will never leave or forsake us. This is the key to enduring trials and temptations—with every breath, praise the Lord.

The apostle Paul demonstrated this countless times as he went from country to country, city to city, preaching "Christ and Him crucified" (1 Corinthians 2:2). There were times when Paul would arrive in a city and find himself in jail before nightfall. He probably never asked, "Where's the best hotel?" More than likely he asked, "What kind of jail do you have?" because that's where he usually wound up. You might say he had the first flourishing prison ministry. But to our benefit, it was from various jail cells that we have the treasured prison epistles. Paul had fire in his soul for the lost and paid the cost—not so much for the freedom of speech but for the freedom to preach.

Dr. Luke, who traveled extensively with Paul, records one such scene. In the heart of Philippi, Macedonia, Paul and his companion Silas were thrown in jail for healing a young girl who was demon possessed. God's servants were bound; their feet fastened in stocks.

Then at midnight the most beautiful sound filtered through dungeon corridors. It was quite different from the wailing normally heard. Paul and Silas were singing hymns of praise to God. The Bible says that "the prisoners were listening to them" (Acts 16:25). Oh, how God-honoring music soothes the spirit and draws others to Him.

I wonder which of the psalms they sang. Perhaps they were there long enough to sing them all. The inmates could have heard these and more:

> In God (I will praise his word) . . .
> I will not fear.
> What can flesh do to me? (Psalm 56:4)

> Bring my soul out of prison,
> That I may praise Your name. (142:7)

Suddenly, the foundation of the prison was shaken. A great earthquake had caused the doors to swing open, and the prisoners' chains fell off (Acts 16:26). Imagine the chaos and free-for-all that resulted. Scripture tells us that the prison guard rushed into the darkness; he could barely see the doors opened wide.

He drew his sword to kill himself because he knew he would be severely punished for the great escape. Then he heard, "Do yourself no harm, for we are all here" (v. 28). It was the voice of Paul. The guard found a light and discovered that no one had escaped. In fact, they willingly submitted to him. In disbelief, the guard humbled himself and fell down trembling before Paul and Silas and said, "Sirs, what must I do to be saved?" (v. 30). This man had heard the Gospel of praise from the prison cell of Paul and Silas, and his heart was moved to salvation because Paul and Silas gave glory and honor to the Lord in the midst of their trials.

> Then they believed His words;
> They sang His praise. (Psalm 106:12)

What rich blessings we receive from the Word of God. James urges us to praise in suffering (James 5:13). Throughout the New Testament Paul referred to the "praise of . . . His grace" (Ephesians 1:6), the "praise of His glory" (v. 12), praise with the brethren (Hebrews 2:12), and the "sacrifice of praise" (13:15). And in his second Corinthian letter, he referred to one of God's faithful as "the brother whose praise is in the gospel" (8:18). What a testimony to have among fellow Christians!

Peter referred to this blessing with eternity in mind: "praise . . . at the revelation of Jesus Christ" (1 Peter 1:7), praise "of Him who called you out of darkness into His marvelous light" (2:9), and glorifying God "through Jesus Christ" with praise "forever" (4:11).

All these men of God praised Him in the face of death, and unto death, as they each died as martyrs for the sake of and the eternal praise of Jesus Christ.

What will praise sound like in Heaven eternal? We will no longer sing praises in the midst of persecution, despair, or imprisonment, for "He has put a new song in my mouth," a song of praise to God (Psalm 40:3).

We will praise Him in His mighty expanse. We will sing praise to the most High and praise His power. We will praise Him for His Word. And one day His holy name will be praised by everything that has breath.

The LORD shall reign forever . . .
Praise the LORD! (Psalm 146:10)

CHAPTER 24

Righteousness Forever

The Everlasting Foundation

1 and 2 Corinthians

Awake to righteousness.

—1 Corinthians 15:34

His righteousness endures **forever**.

—2 Corinthians 9:9

Staying youthful was always a goal of mine. Nothing in me was attracted to old things, not even to my wife's beloved antiques. When I was young, I could not imagine being old. I had an unusual amount of energy, and it followed me into young adulthood. When middle age set in, I dealt with physical weariness, but my mind was always in high gear, and it never took long for my physical stamina to return after a grueling schedule. I fought growing old every way I could, faithfully exercising and pacing myself as I began to feel the grasp of Old Man Time. This was not a transition I welcomed, and at one point I began to dread what I knew was coming.

My wife, Ruth, however, was one of those who could lighten heavy hearts, especially mine. I'll never forget when she announced what she wanted on her gravestone, and those who have so graciously visited her gravesite at the Billy Graham Library have seen that she got her way.

Long before Ruth became bedridden, she was driving along a highway through a construction site. Carefully following the detours and mile-by-mile cautionary signs, she came to the last one that said, "End of Construction. Thank You for Your Patience."

She arrived home that day chuckling and told the family about the postings. "When I die," she said, "I want that engraved on my stone." She was lighthearted but serious about her request. She even wrote it out so that we wouldn't forget.

While we appreciated the humor, we also found the truth she conveyed through those few words enlightening. Every human being is under construction from conception to death. Each life is made up of mistakes and learning, waiting and growing, practicing patience and being persistent. At the end of construction—death—we have completed the process.

The age-old question flashes in our minds: "Is that it?" Not at all.

People in Bible times asked the same question, and Paul wrote, "If in this life only we have hope in Christ, we are of all men most miserable. But now is Christ risen from the dead, and become the firstfruits of them that slept" (1 Corinthians 15:19–20 KJV).

Paul made it clear in Scripture that just as Adam brought death to all men through sin, so Christ can make men alive through the cross and the resurrection.

Physical death says, "This is the finality of accomplishment." We cannot add anything more to our earthly experience. The natural body is earthbound, created from the dust of the ground, and designed to live for an appointed time. It cannot inherit what will last forever.

The spirit (the soul), however, belongs to the God who breathed into it life. This is the real part that has been under construction. This is what makes us the individuals we are—the unseen properties of personality, thoughts, and emotions. The psalmist wrote,

> I will praise You, for I am fearfully and wonderfully made;
> Marvelous are Your works,
> And that my soul knows very well. (Psalm 139:14)

When, as believers in Christ, we strive to live righteously, aided by the Holy Spirit, we die as believers in Christ, who then makes us righteous.

> He restores my soul;
> He leads me in the paths of righteousness
> For His name's sake. (23:3)

The first man, Adam, represents the natural body. But the last Adam—that is, Christ—is a "life-giving Spirit" (1 Corinthians 15:45) who represents the spiritual body. The natural man reaps unrighteousness, and the spiritual man reaps righteousness. The unbeliever loves the things of the world, and the believer loves the things of God. Let's look at these two bodies that war against one another.

The natural man is a lover of the things of the flesh and seeks ways to satisfy his carnal cravings by running after pleasure and feeding his sensuality. The natural man is rebellious, deceitful, and blind. He doesn't want to be controlled because he is a lover of self. The natural man simply does not seek God. We are all born with these tendencies, and when they are fed, they lead people to death.

> As righteousness leads to life,
> So he who pursues evil pursues it to his own death.
> (Proverbs 11:19)

Not far from where I live, a local bank was robbed. The thief demanded cash from the teller, but he didn't know that the bag she handed to him contained a dye bomb. It exploded, covering the money, the bag, and his hand. The law judged him because of the irrefutable evidence against him.

Because of sin, we have dye that has blackened our souls, and we can't wash it off. We're left with stains that will be revealed in the judgment. The only cleanser that will wash it pure as snow is the crimson blood of Jesus Christ, which gives believers a righteous standing before God. The Bible says, "not having my own righteousness, which is from the law, but that which is through faith in Christ, the righteousness which is from God by faith" (Philippians 3:9).

God has planted in us the capacity to know Him. When we accept Christ, the spiritual man is made new and given the Holy Spirit to change his nature, causing him to dwell on things that are righteous and holy. The spiritually minded become "partakers of the divine nature" (2 Peter 1:4). This doesn't mean believers never have temptations, but believers are given strength to turn away from them and live in the way that pleases God.

The apostle Paul spent a great deal of time writing to the church at Corinth. To me, the Corinthian church was one of the saddest and most tragic churches in the New Testament. Those who served and worshiped there were fleshly and unspiritual. In Paul's first letter to them he wrote, "And I, brethren, could not speak to you as to spiritual people but as to carnal, as to babes in Christ. . . . Are you not carnal and behaving like mere men?" (1 Corinthians 3:1–3). He continued, "Do you not know that you are the temple of God and that the Spirit of God dwells in you? If anyone defiles the temple of God, God will destroy him. For the temple of God is holy" (vv. 16–17).

In love, Paul corrected the Corinthian Christians and instructed them that unless they were continually filled with the Holy Spirit, their service would not be empowered with strength from above. His words of discipline must have been difficult to hear, even though they were necessary. "Now no chastening seems to be joyful for the present, but painful; nevertheless, afterward it yields the peaceable fruit of righteousness to those who have been trained by it" (Hebrews 12:11).

Just as we feed the physical body, we must also feed the soul. How do we do this? By an act of the will in obedience to the Spirit, allowing God to plant seeds of truth from His Word, which brings the power. We must acknowledge the presence of the Holy Spirit that indwells us, praying for God's Word to instruct us and asking Him to give us wisdom to obey Him. This empowers our faith. "The . . . righteous know what is acceptable" (Proverbs 10:32). This is how to increase the "fruits of . . . righteousness" (2 Corinthians 9:10).

Through Adam's sin of disobedience all were made sinners; "so also by one Man's obedience," His sacrifice on the cross for sin, "many will be made righteous" (Romans 5:19). Peter wrote to believers "that we, having died to sins, might live for righteousness" (1 Peter 2:24).

Being raised to new life is best explained by the principles of planting crops. I grew up on a farm and learned to work the land. A seed has life in it, but when planted, it first must die then be restored to produce fruit.

This is the picture of death and resurrection. The bodies of believers die to the carnal life and are raised anew. The Bible says, "But God gives it a body as He pleases, and to each seed its own body" (1 Corinthians 15:38).

My wife, Ruth, walked with me along the path of life for sixty-four years, and I miss her. She was the most godly woman I have ever known. She followed Christ along the pathway He marked out for her with grace and dignity, and she smiled through the journey—good or bad. How many times I have heard her quote 2 Corinthians 5:1: "For we know that if our earthly house, this tent, is destroyed, we have a building from God, a house not made with hands, eternal in the heavens."

When Ruth was separated from her pain-stricken body, and her earthly construction was complete, she found lasting peace. Her dwelling now is eternal.

The memories are vivid as I recall her last moments with us at her beloved Little Piney Cove, our home in the Blue Ridge Mountains. Her earthly tent was weak and fragile, but her spirit was strong because her mind was on her heavenly home. Her feet, though weary, were ready to take the first step into Glory. She no longer has detours to maneuver; she has traveled the smooth highway to Heaven. I will join her soon.

My wife loved old things; they represented longevity, character, and survival. This love for the old made her treasure childhood memories from China. When Ruth died, the family had the Chinese character for righteousness engraved on a very old stone. She had looked forward to the day she would stand before the Lord, having awakened to righteousness—a godly attribute older than time.

As Christians we can look forward to standing in the righteousness of Christ because the Good News is the Gospel of old that is from the beginning and will forever endure.

But the righteous has an everlasting
foundation. (Proverbs 10:25)

CHAPTER 25

THE CROSS EVERLASTING

The Beam in the Rubble and the Cross in Our Hearts

GALATIANS

> *For he who sows to his flesh will of the flesh reap*
> *corruption, but he who sows to the Spirit will of the*
> *Spirit reap* **everlasting** *life. . . .*
> *But God forbid that I should boast except in the*
> *cross of our Lord Jesus Christ.*

—GALATIANS 6:8, 14

"WE THOUGHT THE DEVIL WAS HERE," SAID THE FIREFIGHTER, "BUT WITH THIS CROSS, WE KNOW GOD IS HERE."[1] Among the rubble in the aftermath of 9/11, a twenty-foot steel-beam cross was uncovered. Though people from many walks of life watched in terror as the World Trade Center towers in New York collapsed, the sight of a cross brought hope to many—and terror to some. Atheists demanded that the cross, later displayed, be removed from the privately operated

National September 11 Memorial and Museum. They claimed that many people were "injured" when they saw it.

To some the cross of Christ brings cheer; to others it incites fear. The cross can be of comfort to people's spirits, or it can reveal the corruption of the human heart and bring conviction of sin. This is an illustration of what the apostle Paul spoke of when he said, "But God forbid that I should boast except in the cross of our Lord Jesus Christ, by whom the world has been crucified to me, and I to the world" (Galatians 6:14).

Paul's message of the Gospel was centered on Jesus Christ and the cross that He bore for the whole world. Paul could have gloried in many things about himself. He was highly educated, a religious scholar and theologian of the Scripture, a Roman citizen with impeccable ancestry, and a skilled orator.

Paul could have also gloried in his encounter with the incarnate Christ on the Damascus Road and the healing of his blindness. He could have gloried in the healing powers he possessed. He could have even gloried in his call to preach to the Gentile world.

But instead Paul gloried in the cross. Why?

Jesus' crucifixion on the cross was the most terrible of all deaths, but Paul understood what the cross represented, and that message fueled his resolve to go into the world and preach the Gospel of Christ. Paul understood the twofold message of the cross of Christ—God's judgment on sin and His great love for the sinner. Paul gloried in the duplicity of what the cross represented.

You see, the cross shows the depth of our sins. We cannot know how deeply sin offends God until we look at the cross. People today look at the cross as a symbol of forgiveness, without considering the sin that put Christ there. The cross, without its powerful message, is powerless.

When you hang a beautiful cross around your neck or pin it on your lapel, let it always remind you that sin sent Jesus Christ to the cross. Let it remind you of the tremendous gift that it brings, but never forget that it was because of our sin that Christ had to die there. And never underestimate the destructive power of sin:

Sin affects the mind. "The natural man does not receive the things of the Spirit of God . . . because they are spiritually discerned" (1 Corinthians 2:14).

Sin affects the will. People easily become slaves to their sins. But Jesus said that His truth will set us free (John 8:32).

Sin affects the conscience. The Bible says, "And their conscience, being weak, is defiled" (1 Corinthians 8:7).

Paul gloried in the cross because it demonstrates God's judgment on sin through the willing sacrifice of Christ on behalf of sinful man.

> We have turned, every one, to his own way;
> And the LORD has laid on Him the iniquity of us all.
>   (Isaiah 53:6)

But he also gloried in the cross because it shows the love of God. "For God so loved the world that He gave His only begotten Son" (John 3:16). But there are other reasons Paul gloried in the cross.

Paul gloried in the cross because it is the only way to salvation. "For there is no other name under heaven given among men by which we must be saved" (Acts 4:12).

Paul gloried in the cross because it gave a new dynamic to life. "Old things have passed away; behold, all things have become new" (2 Corinthians 5:17).

Paul gloried in the cross because he knew it guaranteed the future life. "God has given us eternal life, and this life is in His Son" (1 John 5:11).

Paul gloried in the cross because Christ defeated death by His resurrection. "Everyone who sees the Son and believes in Him may have everlasting life; and I will raise him up at the last day" (John 6:40).

The cross is the meeting place between God and man, and Jesus is the bridge. "For He Himself is our peace . . . and has broken down the middle wall of separation . . . that He might reconcile them both to God in one body through the cross" (Ephesians 2:14-16).

The cross is also the symbol of forgiveness. "Father, forgive them, for they do not know what they do" (Luke 23:34).

The cross represents reconciliation. "But now in Christ Jesus you who once were far off have been brought near by the blood of Christ" (Ephesians 2:13).

The cross represents God's peace. "For it pleased the Father that in Him all the fullness should dwell, and by Him to reconcile all things to Himself, by Him, whether things on earth or things in heaven, having made peace through the blood of His cross" (Colossians 1:19-20).

The cross represents victory over the flesh. "You once walked according to the course of this world . . . and were by nature children of wrath. . . . But God, who is rich in mercy, because of His great love . . . made us alive together with Christ" (Ephesians 2:2–5).

Once you've been to the cross, you can never be the same, and you will never be ashamed of what Jesus Christ has done for you.

The work of Christ on the cross is eternal. Its glory will never fade. The cross was in the heart of the Father and the Son from the beginning, and the Lord did not leave the cross behind when He left this world. The cross is also in the hearts of those who have committed themselves to the Lord.

The tree of life was planted in the garden long ago. It was not uprooted because of man's sin. No, man was uprooted—removed from the tree's life-giving power. Jesus came to restore the power by putting the cross into the hearts of people. That is why Jesus said, "If anyone desires to come after Me, let him . . . take up his cross, and follow Me" (Matthew 16:24).

The cross—His cross—is eternal in its judgment. Moreover, it is eternal by the love it sheds in the hearts of His people. This is why Paul said he would glory only in the cross (Galatians 6:14 KJV). This is why he told us to sow to the Spirit that reaps everlasting life (v. 8).

We cannot just look at the cross as an emblem, as some did in the aftermath of 9/11. The cross must bring us to a decision. Will we cling to it and carry it in our hearts, sowing its message of love and new life, or will we allow the life-giving message to be buried in the rubble of sin, bringing judgment? Will you reap the eternal life of glory, or eternal life bound in shame?

The eternal destination for believers in Christ is the glory of Heaven, provided by the glory of the cross of Him who died for the world. Do not cling to the well-polished cross on display. Cling to the old rugged cross that is bloodstained, for it is the way by which our sinful hearts are washed whiter than snow.

Looking unto Jesus, the author and finisher of our faith,
who for the joy that was set before Him
endured the cross, despising the shame,
and has sat down at the right hand of the throne of God. (Hebrews 12:2)

THE CHURCH ETERNAL

————— *Wake Up and Take Charge* —————

EPHESIANS

> *God's purpose in all this was to use the church to*
> *display his wisdom in its rich variety to all. . . . This*
> *was his* **eternal** *plan.*
>
> —EPHESIANS 3:10–11 NLT

THE CHURCH IS IN TURMOIL TODAY. Why is this? Perhaps it is because the church is spending more time learning worldly ways than learning the Word. I fear that thousands of churches are leading people astray theologically. This leads to spiritual and moral decay, and people are left drifting aimlessly without compass or guide.

God did not ordain this for His church. The Israelites knew what it was to wander, for they wandered in the wilderness forty years. But God's church was called to witness. Yet we see today a great wandering, a defection from the faith, mirroring the pattern of God's ancient people.

> They shall wander . . .
> Seeking the word of the Lord,
> But shall not find it. (Amos 8:12)

The book of Revelation contains seven letters dictated to John to be sent to the seven churches in Asia. Pastors today would do well to take up a serious study of these with their congregations. "He who has an ear, let him hear what the Spirit says to the churches" (Revelation 2:11).

Christ's examination of His churches at that time is also an indictment on the church today. While His words sting with truth, they are also full of wonderful promises of what can happen when we heed His warnings and follow His commands, which bring conviction, repentance, and purification. Only then can the church really be effective.

A man in Oregon once wrote, "For two thousand years the church has been in existence, and we still have war and misery. The church is a failure." I would ask him this: Is penicillin a failure when a patient refuses to accept and follow its directions? Are sulfa drugs a failure when the physician neglects to prescribe them?

The church—the body of Christ—will never fail; however, when "churches" turn away from God's Word to chase after the worldly system, they stumble and fall. There is a vast difference between godliness and worldliness. There is a crisis today of many professing Christians walking hand-in-hand with the world, making it difficult to distinguish the Christian from the unbeliever. This should never be.

The church was not designed to stop wars or to solve misery. The church was designed to proclaim God's love and forgiveness to all people and declare that Jesus Christ came to eradicate sin in people's hearts. He returned to His Father in Heaven to make intercession for us, leaving the church to be His light in a dark and hostile world. There will always be skeptics, but Jesus said, "I will build My church, and the gates of [Hell] shall not prevail against it" (Matthew 16:18).

Today's Christians are beset by worldly propaganda that is infiltrating the church when the things of Jesus Christ should be infusing the church. Years ago on a Sunday morning in Washington, DC, a woman called the National Presbyterian Church, where my good friend, the late Dr. Edward L. R. Elson, pastored. It happened to be the home church of President Eisenhower. The caller asked, "Do you expect the President to be in church today?"

The operator replied, "I cannot promise, but God will be here among His people, and that should be incentive enough for anybody to come." Friends, the church is to be centered on the Lord Jesus Christ.

But what exactly is the church? Is it a building with a steeple or an abandoned sports arena that has been turned into a worship center? Is it an old sanctuary filled with wooden pews or a storefront stocked with folding chairs that can be removed to make room for cultural events? Is church a place of prayer or community service?

What is the true church? One of the Greek words for church, *ekklésia*, means "the called-out ones"[1]—called out of the world, yet to be the light of Christ. This is troubling for many because as they strive to take God's Word to unbelievers, they are often more influenced by the ways of the world.

The church belongs to Jesus Christ. He founded the church. He is the great cornerstone and the foundation upon which it is built (Ephesians 2:20). The church does not belong to pastors or congregations but to Christ alone. It is His dwelling place on earth, through the lives of His followers. We have no right to bring worldly ways into His church. The world's sewage system threatens to contaminate the stream of Christian thought; its roots are taking hold in many churches today.

Paul laid this out in his letter to the church at Ephesus: "Let your roots grow down into him, and let your lives be built on him. Then your faith will grow strong in the truth" (Colossians 2:7 NLT). God's purpose in all of this, Paul said, is to "display his wisdom in its rich variety to all. . . . This was his eternal plan, which he carried out through Christ Jesus our Lord" (Ephesians 3:10–11 NLT).

Jesus died for the church and is over the church. "He is the head of the body, the church . . . that in all things He may have the preeminence" (Colossians 1:18). If we were to examine church programs today, would Christ really be preeminent? Believers should reflect Christ in every way. What a responsibility. What a privilege!

The church is to be built up in His Word. Unless the church quickly recovers the authoritative biblical message, we may witness the spectacle of millions of Christians going outside the institutional church to find spiritual food. To some degree this is already happening, and the Bible gives warning (Hebrews 6:4-6).

Many churches now mold their programs around the community—not the Word of God. Church bulletins often reflect this by announcing grand programs and activities with little to no emphasis on God's Word. The Lord did not design the church to cater to people's wishes—the Lord breathed life into the church to learn, proclaim, and live out His truths. We are to build one another up in the Word of God (Jude 20).

The church is to fellowship together. When Jesus birthed the church, believers submitted to the teaching of the apostles—the inspired Word of God. They also joined in fellowship together, prayed together, and shared the Lord's Supper (Acts 2:42). For them, this fellowship was a taste of Heaven on earth. This is God's eternal design. "[Jesus] is the one who is eternal life. . . . And our fellowship is with the Father and with his Son, Jesus Christ" (1 John 1:2–3 NLT).

The church's message is Jesus Christ crucified, risen, and coming again. Take time to read the Acts of the Apostles; these believers were on fire with the Gospel message. As people observed their witness for Christ, they shouted, "These . . . have turned the world upside down" (Acts 17:6). Is the church today making that kind of impact? Or has it become complacent like the church at Laodicea, whom the Lord rebuked by saying, "You are lukewarm, and neither cold nor hot" (Revelation 3:16)?

Have you ever observed coals in a fire pit? If you remove them and separate them, they will cool and die quickly, but if they are together they stay red hot. Jeremiah said, "Is not My word like a fire?" (Jeremiah 23:29). The body of Christ must be fueled with passion to live testimonies before a dying world.

The church's mission is to make Jesus Christ known. Philip is the only person in the Bible who was called an evangelist. Making Christ known is not a command exclusively given to preachers. I believe one of the greatest priorities of the church is to mobilize the laity to do the work of proclaiming the Gospel. Why? God has His people everywhere. Living the Word of God is what draws people to Christ, but instead, we are using clever gimmicks. We are to be witnesses for Him wherever we are, whatever we are doing.

We see the wonderful example of Priscilla and Aquila, close friends of Paul's. They were tentmakers by trade. But they also acted as leaders in the church and effective witnesses for Christ in their world, using every opportunity to tell others about the Way (the name of the church in the book of Acts; see Acts 9:2). Likewise, Christ has given each of us our role, and He expects us to obey and serve Him. If we do not walk in the way Christ commands, then we cannot point out the Way to others.

The church must be prepared to endure persecution. Paul said that we should prepare for hardship as good soldiers. "No one engaged in warfare entangles himself with the affairs of this life," he wrote to Timothy (2 Timothy 2:4).

Paul also wrote, "Be strong in the Lord and in the power of His might. Put on the whole armor of God, that you may be able to stand against the wiles of the devil" (Ephesians 6:10–11). We are told to be prepared—to wear the belt of truth, put on the breastplate of righteousness, pull on the boots that will carry the Gospel, and take up the shield of faith, the helmet of salvation, and the sword of the Spirit (the Word of God), which represents Christ's entire message. And we are to keep in mind that this battle is not ours, but God's (2 Chronicles 20:15).

The Army Rangers is a distinguished regiment—a special training force. I am fascinated to hear my grandson, an Army Ranger, describe the intense training it takes to be combat ready. The Rangers have one objective: to become tough, fit, and ready to defend freedom.

This is a picture of what the church should be as well—fit and ready to battle sin in Jesus' name and fight the good fight of faith. "Pursue righteousness, godliness, faith, love, patience, gentleness. Fight the good fight of faith, lay hold on eternal life, to which you were also called" (1 Timothy 6:11–12).

The eternal reward for the church's faithfulness is promised:

"Because you have kept My command to persevere, I also will keep you from the hour of trial which shall come upon the whole . . . earth. Behold, I am coming quickly! Hold fast what you have, that no one may take your crown. He who overcomes, I will make him a pillar in the temple of My God, and he shall go out no more." (Revelation 3:10–12)

The church is the bride of Christ. This description may seem strange, but it is the relationship God had in mind in the beginning. When God took a rib from Adam's side and formed the woman, Adam's bride, this was a picture of what was to come—the church as the bride of Christ. When Christ finished His great work on the cross and gave up His spirit, a soldier pierced His side, and the blood that was shed gave birth to the church of the living God.

Not only is the church the bride of Christ, but the members of His body become "joint heirs with Christ" and the children of God (Romans 8:17).

That glorious day is coming when we will be caught up in the air with our Bridegroom, Jesus Christ. The bride of Christ is the triumphant and eternal church, which will be gathered to His side and reign with Him forever. The angels will sing, instruments will resound; God's people will praise and worship the Redeemer. What a day that will be for the church eternal!

To Him be glory in the church by Christ Jesus
to all generations, forever and ever. (Ephesians 3:21)

CHAPTER 27

ETERNAL GLORY

Honoring the Holy

PHILIPPIANS, COLOSSIANS

My God shall supply all your need according to His riches in glory. . . . **forever and ever.**

—PHILIPPIANS 4:19–20

Set your mind on things above. . . . When Christ who is our life appears, then you also will appear with Him in glory.

—COLOSSIANS 3:2, 4

PEOPLE HAVE TWO GREAT SPIRITUAL NEEDS. The first is forgiveness, which God has made possible by sending His Son into the world to die for our sins. Our second need is goodness, which God also made possible by sending the Holy Spirit to dwell within us while still on earth. We actually have the glory of the Lord with us in this life because His Spirit abides in us. Do we really comprehend that the Lord of all gives us a taste of His abundant attributes while we are still in these earthly bodies? Do our lives reflect this?

As needy people we ask the Lord for many things: food, clothing, jobs, homes, a spouse, children, and more. Our minds are focused on our physical needs when the Bible tells us not to worry about such things (Matthew 6:25-34). Instead, Paul prays that the Holy Spirit will guide us in all truth and wisdom. "I pray that from his glorious, unlimited resources he will empower you with inner strength through his Spirit. Then Christ will make his home in your hearts as you trust in him" (Ephesians 3:16–17 NLT). This is a wonderful promise.

It helps to remember that God the Father, God the Son, and God the Holy Spirit have all existed from eternity. The Trinity is identified in the first chapter of Scripture: "Then God said, 'Let Us make man in Our image, according to Our likeness'" (Genesis 1:26). The work of creation was given to the Son (John 1:3), and the Holy Spirit was moving upon the face of His Creation (Genesis 1:2).

The Father is the source of all blessing. The Son is the channel of all blessing. And it is through the Holy Spirit at work in us that all truth becomes living and operative in our lives. "We . . . are being transformed into the same image from glory to glory, just as by the Spirit of the Lord" (2 Corinthians 3:18).

If Christians realized that God Himself in the Person of the Holy Spirit really dwells within our bodies, we would be far more careful about what we eat, drink, look at, or read. Can we really fool ourselves by saying, "Lord, I am going to see a movie that has inappropriate content, but please give me a spiritual blessing as I watch this and help my life be a witness for You"? Or can we honestly ask the Lord to bless any activity that is dishonoring to Him by excusing it with "I need to relate to my friends"?

The Lord commands us to come out from the worldly system and be separate. This does not mean that we should never associate with the world, but we are not to partake of the things the world engages in that cannot bring glory to God. This command should drive us to our knees in confession and obedience.

It pleases the Lord that His people would desire the more important things. We are called to be His examples on earth. Do we conduct ourselves like God's ambassadors, His children, or Christ's bride? Do we turn our backs on feeding the flesh? The Holy Spirit gives liberty to the Christian, direction to the worker, discernment to the teacher, power to the Word, and fruit for faithful service.

I am deeply concerned when I hear Christians praying for the Holy Spirit to come and "do something." If you know Christ, you don't need to beg for the Holy Spirit to come into your life. He is already there— whether you feel His presence or not. Don't confuse the Holy Spirit with an emotional feeling or a particular type of spiritual experience. It is never a question of how much you and I have of the Spirit, but of how much He has of us. Your body is the home of the Holy Spirit (1 Corinthians 6:19).

It is my belief that a person who is filled with the Spirit may not even be conscious of it. Not one of Christ's followers said of himself, "I am filled with the Spirit." Others said it about them, but they did not claim it for themselves. My friend, the late Roy Gustafson, once said, "The Holy Spirit didn't come to make us Holy-Spirit-conscious but Christ-conscious." Are we?

When Jesus told His disciples that He was going away, He said, "When the Helper comes, whom I shall send to you from the Father, the Spirit of truth who proceeds from the Father, He will testify of Me" (John 15:26). Likewise, we as Christ's followers are to bear witness of Him, so we must be so careful not to seek the Holy Spirit's filling for selfish reasons. The Holy Spirit did not come to glorify us. He did not come to glorify Himself. He came to glorify Christ forever—through us.

You may ask, "How can we glorify Christ?" By living for Him—trusting, loving, obeying, and serving Him, and relying on the Spirit's power to do it. Jesus said, "Let your light so shine before men, that they may see your good works and glorify your Father in heaven" (Matthew 5:16). We cannot glorify Him in the energy of the flesh. Only in the power of the Spirit can we live lives that glorify God, for it is through the Holy Spirit that Christ is glorified in us (Philippians 1:19-20).

Peter is a good example of this. He had been arrested for preaching and was brought before the religious leaders. The Scripture says that Peter, "filled with the Holy Spirit" (Acts 4:8), fearlessly proclaimed the death and resurrection of Christ. Earlier in Scripture, though, we saw this same Peter deny Jesus with curses. What made the difference? The fullness of the Holy Spirit of God. And the result brought glory to the Lord. "When they saw the boldness of Peter and John . . . they marveled. And they realized that they had been with Jesus" (v. 13). What could be filled with more glory than having "been with Jesus"?

The Gospel accounts magnify the glory of Christ, which brings us hope and increases our anticipation of spending eternity with Him. If we do not yearn for God, we either do not possess Christ as our Savior, or we are not feeding our souls with spiritual truth from God's Word. Those who have followed Christ "will appear with Him in glory" (Colossians 3:4). Just hearing His name calls for glorious celebration.

Think of how the New Testament opens, with the most glorious event—when Jesus was born. The angels appeared to shepherds in the field to announce the Good News.

> The glory of the Lord shone around them. . . . Then the angel said to them . . . "I bring you good tidings of great joy which will be to all people. For there is born to you this day in the city of David a Savior, who is Christ the Lord." . . .
> Suddenly there was with the angel a multitude of the heavenly host praising God and saying:
>
> "Glory to God in the highest,
> And on earth peace, goodwill toward men!"
>   (Luke 2:9–14)

When Jesus was baptized by John, the heavens were opened, and "the Holy Spirit descended in bodily form like a dove upon Him." Then the voice of God spoke from Heaven, saying, "You are My beloved Son; in You I am well pleased" (3:22).

Just before Jesus completed His earthly ministry, He took Peter, James, and John up on a mountain to pray. The disciples noticed that the appearance of His face changed, and His robe became white and glistening. They saw Him in all of His glory as they heard the voice from the heavens say again, "This is My beloved Son" (Matthew 17:5).

When Jesus appeared to the disciples after His resurrection, He led them to a place outside of Bethany and said, "You shall receive power when the Holy Spirit has come upon you; and you shall be witnesses to Me . . . to the end of the earth" (Acts 1:8).

He lifted up His hands and blessed them, then ascended into the clouds. While the disciples looked into the sky, two men stood by them arrayed in white apparel. "Men of Galilee," they said, "why do you stand gazing up into heaven? This same Jesus, who was taken up from you into heaven, will so come in like manner as you saw Him go into heaven" (vv. 10–11).

There is coming a day, my friends, when Jesus will appear in the air and all of the earth will see "the Son of Man [coming] in His glory, and all the holy angels with Him, then He will sit on the throne of His glory" (Matthew 25:31). Those who have denied Christ and His holy words will suffer the judgment of the Lord. But even so, every creature who has ever been born will bow before Jesus Christ and confess that He is Lord, "to the glory of God the Father" (Philippians 2:11).

So what are we to do until then? Glorify Him through the proclamation of the Gospel and live in a way that demonstrates the glory of the Holy Spirit that reigns in our lives. "In his kindness God called you to share in his eternal glory by means of Christ Jesus" (1 Peter 5:10 NLT).

We are told many times in the Bible to look for Christ's return, and one day we will behold Him. An angel took the apostle John to a high mountain, and there he saw the holy city of Jerusalem, descending from Heaven in great glory:

> But I saw no temple in it, for the Lord God Almighty and the Lamb are its temple. The city had no need of the sun or of the moon to shine in it, for the glory of God illuminated it. The Lamb is its light. And the nations of those who are saved shall walk in its light, and the kings of the earth bring their glory and honor into it. (Revelation 21:22–24)

We cannot begin to comprehend the glory of it all. The psalmist declared that His name is forever glorious (Psalm 72:19 NLT). Paul said that His kingdom and power is glorious and will be glorified in the church forever (Ephesians 3:21), and James called Jesus the Lord of glory (James 2:1). We can be eternity-minded today as we live to glorify Him.

May the God of all grace, who called us to His
eternal glory by Christ Jesus . . . settle you.
To Him be the glory . . . forever and ever. (1 Peter 5:10–11)

CHAPTER 28

Forever Separated or Forever United

Land of the Lost or Land of the Living

1 and 2 Thessalonians

The believers who have died. . . . [and] we who are still alive and remain. . . . will be with the Lord **forever.**

—1 Thessalonians 4:16–17 NLT

Those who don't know God. . . . will be . . . **forever** *separated from the Lord.*

—2 Thessalonians 1:8–9 NLT

I DIDN'T SAY IT; GOD SAID IT—ALL PEOPLE ARE LOST WITHOUT HIM! Sin is what separates us from God and causes us to wander far from Him. But we don't have to remain there. We don't have to spend eternity in the land of the lost.

201

"Well," you may say, "I do for others. I live a pretty good life."

Consider carefully what God has said: "Our [good works] are like filthy rags" (Isaiah 64:6). Our works will never get us to Heaven. "For by grace you have been saved through faith, and that not of yourselves; it is the gift of God, not of works, lest anyone should boast" (Ephesians 2:8–9).

Life and death come to the body and soul. The Bible says, "Do not fear those who kill the body but cannot kill the soul. But rather fear Him who is able to destroy both soul and body in hell" (Matthew 10:28).

The worst kind of death is described in Scripture—unending death in a lake of fire and brimstone that burns forever. Just as we cannot fathom the wonder of living forever in glory, we cannot possibly comprehend the alternative.

Greek scholar A. T. Robertson said, "Gather all the expressions you can find in the New Testament, such as *Hell, lake of fire, outer darkness*, and *bottomless pit*, and let your imagination run wild, and it will be impossible for you to ever understand the awfulness of what it means to be lost."

Every person who rejects Christ and His atoning work will be cast into this horrible pit of despair. Worse will be to remember that it was by choice—that God called you to salvation but you rejected His wonderful gift. God does not send unrepentant souls into the pit of darkness; those souls choose their destiny. You've heard the saying, "They aren't living; they are just existing!" There will be "no purposeful living" in Hell, just an existence beyond all misery.

Satan is very much out in the open these days. He is flexing his power of allurement, scattering the broad road with pretty—but deadly—flowers that lead to Hell. Our culture is saturated with devilish humor delivered as amusement. Much of the music glorifies him. Tantalizing movies and reckless television programming feeds boredom. Is it any wonder that nearly all forms of entertainment are filled with demonic trappings?

You may wonder what Hell is really like. Don't look to comedians for answers. The Bible tells you the truth. Hell is a place of sorrow and unrest, a place of wailing and a furnace of fire; a place of torment, a place of outer darkness, a place where people scream for mercy; a place of everlasting punishment.

This is God's description, not mine. And it is where many will spend eternity. If you accept any part of the Bible, you are forced to accept the reality of Hell, the place of punishment for those who reject Christ.

Many people object to the doctrine of Hell. Some believe in universalism—that everyone will eventually be saved. Others do not accept that *eternal* and *everlasting* mean forever. But the same biblical word that speaks of eternal punishment is used for eternal life in Heaven. The same Greek word is used with the *joy of the righteous* and the *punishment of the wicked*; the duration is the same: forever.

Annihilation is another theory about what happens at the end of earthly life—the soul ceases to exist and is destroyed. But when the Bible speaks of perishing, it can be translated as *destruction*, *perdition*, *misery*. These do not mean that the soul ceases to be, but rather it is so ruined that it no longer serves the purpose for which it was designed.

Today the subject of Hell is very popular, except in churches. And I am concerned that many preachers have stopped talking about it since the Lord Himself spoke more about Hell than He did about Heaven, and He didn't sugarcoat His description of this woeful place. Our culture, however, ignores this and has learned to be comfortable with the idea of Hell. Many even brag that they look forward to it.

Jesus told a parable in Luke 16:19–30 about a beggar named Lazarus who died and was carried away by the angels to Abraham's bosom, another way of describing Heaven (v. 23). A rich man who had been cruel to Lazarus also died and was buried, and his soul went to Hades, the place of the dead.

Jesus said that the tormented rich man saw Abraham at a far distance, and Lazarus was with him. The man shouted, "Father Abraham, have mercy on me, and send Lazarus that he may dip the tip of his finger in water and cool my tongue; for I am tormented in this flame" (v. 24). The rich man begged for relief, but there was a great chasm of separation between him and Lazarus; no one could cross over. The rich man then begged Abraham to send someone to warn his brothers so they wouldn't wind up in the land of the lost.

In His story, Jesus used vivid imagery to describe the awfulness of Hell, and He also painted a picture of eternal separation. There is no recourse after death. It is doomsday for unbelievers and reunion day for those in the presence of Christ. There are no appeals.

The "chasm" in the story points to the cross. You see, this is why Jesus came. Through His death and resurrection, Jesus became the bridge for sinners, allowing us to cross over from separation to eternal fellowship with God.

Let's look at this rich man. It is clear in the story that he had physical features. His eyes could see, his ears could hear, his mind was functioning, his memory was recalling his living brothers, his mouth could speak, and his tongue was burning. It is doubtful that this man was thinking about his riches, but if he was, he realized for the first time that money wouldn't buy him a get-out-of-jail-free card.

This man's conscience was fully engaged; he was in mental anguish. He was lonely and hopeless, but still he wanted Lazarus to serve him. There was no sign of humility. Nor did he ask for personal salvation—he had ignored his hour of decision on earth, and he knew there was no turning back. His only redeeming act was to beg someone to warn his brothers not to follow him to the place of terror.

The purpose of Hell is judgment of sin. Sin is the rejection of the Lord Jesus Christ—the remedy for sin. Human beings have an intuitive and instinctive nature; they know when they've gone bad. That's why so much effort is given to covering up bad deeds. The conscience can signal a person when he or she has sinned. Guilt begins to gnaw inside. A little red light in the soul warns of a day of retribution. Now, when people continually sin, they can become immune and no longer notice the warning signs.

Most societies do not permit incorrigible lawbreakers to have the same liberty as law-abiding citizens. Take away law enforcement and retribution for crimes, and lawlessness would be more rampant than it is now.

Few would disagree that there must be consequences for breaking the law. God's law, designed for the whole world, is no different.

Hades, a Greek word, is mentioned ten times in the New Testament and has the same meaning as *Sheol*, a Hebrew word that is used in the Old Testament. Both describe a place of judgment—the underworld of evil, the place of the dead. Either would make any prison in the world look attractive.

But worse than any description is this fact: Hell is eternal separation from the Lord Jesus Christ. It is the second death, described as the eternal conscious banishment from the presence of God.

The Bible warns us not to be deceived:

> But the cowardly, unbelieving, abominable, murderers, sexually immoral, sorcerers, idolaters, and all liars shall have their part in the lake which burns with fire and brimstone, which is the second death. (Revelation 21:8)

People outside of Jesus Christ are headed to that place. "Unless you repent you will all likewise perish" (Luke 13:5).

Did you notice the good news embedded in the little word *unless*? It speaks of God's great mercy toward mankind. The same Bible that teaches the wrath and judgment of God also teaches the longsuffering love of God.

> The LORD is merciful and gracious,
> Slow to anger, and abounding in mercy. (Psalm 103:8)

God hates sin with a holy hatred. As long as you are attached to your sins, you're going to spend eternity in Hell. But thanks be to God, He has provided another way, another destination—Heaven. Why? He loves us and wants "all [to] come to repentance" (2 Peter 3:9).

God the Father does not want anyone to go to Hell. Neither does God the Son. And God the Holy Spirit doesn't want it either. And let me say this: unless you're convicted of your sin, you can never be saved and live as a Christian.

So when you sense a still, small voice in your soul—and you have or you will—it is the Holy Spirit of God telling you that you're not right with Him. Do not ignore the Voice. God is drawing you by His love—don't pull away. When you quench the fire of conviction, you have rejected the Holy Spirit. So when you feel that tug, do not resist. Take hold of the living Christ, who will come and dwell in you.

The only one who wants you in Hell is the devil. He's whispering in your ear, saying, "Don't make a decision for Christ; you've got plenty of time." That is the devil's big lie. The truth is you don't have plenty of time. I cannot find anywhere in Scripture that promises one more minute of life. The Bible says that today is the day of salvation (2 Corinthians 6:2). One of these days the door of grace will close; it will be too late.

The gore of Hell is an indescribable eternity, but the glories of Heaven are too wonderful to visualize. No description of Hell would make anyone want to go there. Cling to the hope of Heaven. Love the One who can grant you entrance.

Christ "has broken down the middle wall of separation" (Ephesians 2:14) so that we can enjoy a personal relationship and eternal fellowship with Him. The worst thing for those confined to Hell will be the eternal separation from the One who built the bridge to Heaven by way of the cross. This Way bypasses the land of the lost and leads directly to the land of the living.

You who were once far away from God. . . .
were . . . separated from him
by your evil thoughts and actions. Yet now
he has reconciled you to himself . . .
[and] has brought you into his own presence. (Colossians 1:21–22 NLT)

CHAPTER 29

SERVING FOR ETERNITY

Complaining or Obeying

1 AND 2 TIMOTHY

*Serve them because those who are benefited are
believers and beloved. . . .*
 *Lay hold on **eternal** life, to which you were also
called.*

—1 TIMOTHY 6:2, 12

I serve with a pure conscience. . . .
 *that they also may obtain the salvation which is
in Christ Jesus with **eternal** glory.*

—2 TIMOTHY 1:3; 2:10

THE PLACE TO START SERVING THE LORD IS RIGHT WHERE YOU
ARE. We sometimes make the mistake of thinking that ministers are the
only ones called of God. But Christians are a "called-out people" with a

specific task—to obey Christ in all things. Serving Him is not a part-time endeavor; we are to serve Him with eternity in mind.

Some set their hearts on fulfilling a dream instead of doing what is obvious. "Serve Him with a loyal heart and with a willing mind" (1 Chronicles 28:9).

Remember Mary, the sister of Martha and Lazarus, who wanted to sit at Jesus' feet to learn from Him? One day Mary was with Jesus and others at the home of Simon the leper. While there, she took an alabaster bottle filled with expensive oil, broke it open, and poured the costly fragrance over the Lord's head. Judas reprimanded her, scolding her that the oil could have been sold for a great deal of money and used to feed the poor. But Jesus spoke in Mary's defense and told the disciples, "You have the poor with you always, but Me you do not have always" (Matthew 26:11).

The disciples' response revealed how little they understood about the Lord's pending death. Many scurry about doing "good works" in hopes that the Lord will see their efforts and reward them, but they fail to live obediently in every other area of life. Our service to others must never replace doing the good thing for the Lord Jesus—putting Him first in the way we live.

Jesus did not hesitate to commend Mary: "She has done what she could. . . . I say to you, wherever this gospel is preached in the whole world, what this woman has done will also be told as a memorial to her" (Mark 14:8–9). How wonderful that Mary's demonstration of service lives into eternity for the Gospel's sake. How? It is documented in the living Book—the Word of God.

The New Testament church was made up primarily of people like Mary who did what they could. Several disciples were fishermen. There is no more effective witness for Christ than for others to see believers dedicated to Jesus Christ in word and deed in all walks of life, doing what they can in His name.

This is exactly what Paul did when he was prevented from traveling to Rome. He wrote the church and said, "For God is my witness, whom I serve with my spirit in the gospel of His Son, that without ceasing I make mention of you always in my prayers" (Romans 1:9). Prayer is an area of serving God that does not get much acclaim. It does not rise to the level of adventure, yet it is the most powerful thing we can do for others and ourselves.

Believers are also called to serve one another. "As we have opportunity, let us do good to all, especially to those who are of the household of faith" (Galatians 6:10). While it is important to reach out to those who do not know the Lord, we must first reach out to those who love Him, encouraging and supporting them as they also serve Christ. Jesus commended those who supported believers and credited their service as though it was done for Him.

"For whoever gives you a cup of water to drink in My name, because you belong to Christ, assuredly, I say to you, he will by no means lose his reward" (Mark 9:41). Many people misunderstand this verse, so it is worth taking a closer look at what Jesus said. Many people believe that true service is only to the lost, but the verse makes it clear that Jesus was commending those who gave to His servants. The household of faith is close to the Lord's heart because it is His body on earth.

Over the three years of Jesus' ministry, He looked forward to being in the home of His friends Lazarus, Mary, and Martha. These siblings loved the Lord and served Him by welcoming Him into their home, providing good meals and sweet fellowship. The Bible says, "Through love serve one another" (Galatians 5:13).

Some believe that they can do God's work only on a mission field far from home. Missionary work is a high calling, but if God called every believer to foreign missions, there would be no Gospel light in our schools, businesses, governments, or churches. Christians at work in the world are the only real spiritual light in the midst of great spiritual darkness. This places a tremendous responsibility on all of us.

A young mother once asked me how she could serve the Lord and was offended when I suggested she serve Him right in her home. She had small children. That was her mission field. Don't look for ways to serve the Lord if it means neglecting the responsibilities you have under your own roof.

An elderly couple had been praying for the Lord to show them how they could serve Him. Physically, they were unable to venture far from home. One day a young mother, their neighbor, knocked at their door and handed them some fresh bread she had baked. The couple, overwhelmed at her gift, invited her in. Looking into her pale face with dark circles under her eyes, they learned she was suffering from a serious disease and asked if they could pray with her. A tear fell on her cheek, and she said, "No one has ever prayed for me before." As the weeks and months passed, the couple came to know the woman and began looking after her children on occasion while the woman went for medical treatment. The couple baked cookies and taught the children Bible stories after school. In time the entire family came to know the Lord. This is service with eternal value. "Do not be ashamed of the testimony of our Lord" (2 Timothy 1:8).

In our world today Christian service is often mistaken for humanitarian service. The important thing to remember is that Christ called His followers to proclaim His message, and this is done in various ways. Ministering to people's souls is far greater than providing only physical needs. Often, however, we earn the opportunity to share Christ when a helpful hand has been extended to someone in need. Then you can say with Paul, "I thank God, whom I serve with a pure conscience" (v. 3).

Then there are some—thank God—who are certain of God's call to service in a foreign land. If this is true of you, take the necessary steps in that direction, and God will confirm that call by opening a door of opportunity. How often I have seen people very sure that this was what God wanted them to do, yet they were not willing to sacrifice or prepare. They had the spirit of adventure, not service.

A few years ago a youth group traveled to the Middle East to help in a small mission hospital. When they arrived in the hot desert, they were disgruntled with the accommodations and the sandstorms that swept through the compound. One evening, when they were asked to prepare medicine packs for patients the next day, they quickly left for the city to find air conditioning and a good time. The nurse at the hospital later told representatives of the church that had sent them, "Please don't send any more help!"

Scripture tells us to "serve the Lord without distraction" (1 Corinthians 7:35). Serving others in the name of Jesus Christ is serious business. It is important to be honest with yourself. Do not say you are serving God if you are serving your selfish desires because God will not bless you. Do not serve others to be praised because God will not bless you.

Then there are those who feel called to preach. To those I say, if you can be content doing anything else, do not go into that area of ministry because preaching must be your passion. My call to preach was the result of a compelling urge to devote myself to the ministry, and as I sought Him in every decision I had to make, God led me each step of the way.

If preaching is approached as just a vocation, it will not be enough to strengthen you for the battles that come with speaking God's Word. There will be obstacles, strife, and many hardships. Being victorious over these onslaughts comes from knowing you are where God has called you. If there is an inner urge to proclaim the message of Christ, then read the Word faithfully, commit your desire to God in prayer, and watch Him work. "So I am willing to endure anything if it will bring salvation and eternal glory in Christ Jesus" (2 Timothy 2:10 NLT).

The Lord demonstrated the truest service when He willingly left the glories of Heaven to live among men, then die for them. Jesus entered into the arena of human troubles. He wept with people and rejoiced with them in their victories. We must do no less. "The Son of Man did not come to be served, but to serve, and to give His life a ransom for many" (Matthew 20:28).

Jesus, by His own example, has shown us how to serve. It does not matter what titles or positions we hold. The Bible clearly teaches that we should be servants—even bondservants—and even more emphasis is given to those in leadership positions. Take the lead by serving.

After Jesus washed the disciples' feet, He said, "If I then, your Lord and Teacher, have washed your feet, you also ought to wash one another's feet" (John 13:14).

The Bible gives us many wonderful promises about Heaven, but one of the greatest is that we shall serve the Father and the Son before the throne (Revelation 22:3). Until that day, may He find us at work for Him so that we can one day hear these wonderful words: "Well done, good and faithful servant; you were faithful over a few things, I will make you ruler over many things. Enter into the joy of your lord" (Matthew 25:21).

Start where you are. Do the few things in your pathway. Be faithful, and God will give the increase.

The invitation to discipleship and serving the Lord is the most thrilling to ever come to God's people. Just imagine being a working partner with God in the redemption of the world.

Christian service, wherever we are, gives us the privilege of being intimately associated with Christ. And the faithful discharging of the responsibilities of true discipleship invokes the approval and favor of God Himself that will have eternal benefits.

If anyone serves Me, let him follow Me; and
where I am, there My servant will be also.
If anyone serves Me, him My Father will honor. (John 12:26)

CHAPTER 30

THE EVERLASTING GOSPEL

Commissioning the Message

TITUS, PHILEMON

Eternal *life which God . . . promised before time began . . . manifested His word through preaching.*

—TITUS 1:2–3

That on your behalf he might minister to me in my chains for the gospel.
   That you might receive him **forever**.

—PHILEMON 13, 15

THE FORCES OF THE DEVIL ARE ASSAULTING THE PEOPLE OF GOD, BUT THE GOSPEL OF THE KINGDOM IS ASSAULTING THE KINGDOM OF SATAN. How? By preaching Christ, which has the power to transform those who are enemies of the cross.

We see this demonstrated in the brief letter to Philemon, a convert of

Paul's and a man who opened his home to the church at Colossae. Paul wrote, "The hearts of the saints have been refreshed by you, brother" (Philemon 7).

Onesimus, a servant of Philemon, had stolen money from him and fled to Rome, where he was converted under Paul's ministry. Paul sent Onesimus back to Philemon, asking him to receive Onesimus both as a man and as a brother in the Lord (v. 16). Paul appealed to the more mature Christian to fully demonstrate the Gospel of Jesus Christ through forgiveness and acceptance of one who was truly repentant.

Likewise, when Paul wrote to Titus, he encouraged and instructed the young preacher concerning evangelizing the lost and growing them up in the Lord.

In my early years of ministry, I learned a great deal by listening to men of God like Donald Grey Barnhouse and Vance Havner. In turn, I have tried to pass on to others what God has taught me, preaching the Gospel without compromising God's truth.

One of the great thrills of my life was to speak to a gathering of itinerant preachers from around the world—a conference that was convened in Amsterdam, Holland, in 1983 (and subsequently in 1986 and 2000). To see these servants of God from many nations of the world with Bibles in hand gave me a sense of the Lord's great calling to those who proclaim His message. Many were young in the ministry; others had known persecution, and some could relate to Paul, who was imprisoned—bound in chains—for the Gospel. But Paul proclaimed, "The word of God is not chained" (2 Timothy 2:9).

Paul's pastoral epistles are treasured by those who are called to preach. Paul knew the enemy and faithfully warned those who preached Christ to live worthy of His message.

Holy living is essential to effective ministry. It does not mean perfect living, for none of us can live a perfect life on earth. *Holy* means "consecrated," a word seldom heard anymore, but which is still very useful. We are to be consecrated to the Lord, set apart for the Lord's service.

The Bible says, "Adorn the doctrine of God our Savior in all things.

For the grace of God that brings salvation has appeared to all men, teaching us that, denying ungodliness and worldly lusts, we should live soberly, righteously, and godly in the present age" (Titus 2:10–12). What a marvelous thought—to "adorn" the doctrine of God in "all things."

Paul warned about those who professed to know God but whose lives did not back up their professions, and they were "disqualified for every good work" (1:16). Preachers are not salesmen, for they have nothing to sell. They are bearers of God's truth. There is no room for compromise.

The conflict of the ages is escalating. People are asking, "What is going on in the world?" Many are in derision. People have abandoned God, but God has not abandoned the world. Scripture tells us that we are to preach the Gospel, "and then the end will come" (Matthew 24:14). Every Christian is to be a witness; every follower of Christ should proclaim His Word. This is why the Lord said, "Occupy till I come" (Luke 19:13 KJV).

Down through the centuries we have seen God's faithful "occupying." Peter preached and urged people to be saved from "this perverse generation" (Acts 2:40). When the infant church was persecuted, believers scattered and preached the Gospel (8:4). Paul persuaded people about Jesus from the Scripture from morning till evening (28:23).

The Gospel is an urgent message. Why? Because of Christ's imminent return. A great many people have been martyred for preaching this message. Today we see the storm clouds, and we must continue occupying so lost souls can escape the judgment of Hell.

The apostle Philip went down to Samaria and "preached the things concerning the kingdom of God" (8:12). What is the Gospel of the kingdom? The message of Christ, who died for our sins, was buried, and was raised from the dead on the third day (1 Corinthians 15:3–4), and all that is taught in Scripture about Him and His eternal plan for the human race.

Jesus has defeated the three enemies of man—sin, Satan, and death. While they are still present in this life, Christ has conquered them all. Paul wrote, "He canceled the record of the charges against us and took it away by nailing it to the cross. . . . He disarmed the spiritual rulers and authorities. He shamed them publicly by his victory over them on the cross" (Colossians 2:14–15 NLT). This is the Good News.

The full manifestation of what Christ has accomplished will be seen when the end comes. Until then, the everlasting Gospel will be preached (Matthew 24:14). It is "everlasting" because of its eternal nature; the Gospel saves to the uttermost (Revelation 14:6).

It is staggering to think that God has entrusted to people like us—redeemed sinners—the responsibility of carrying out His divine purpose. The Bible says, "The word of the truth of the gospel, which has come to you, as it has also in all the world . . . is bringing forth fruit" (Colossians 1:5–6).

We are now closer to finishing this mission than any previous generation has been. I have watched how God has opened doors for the Gospel in some of the most mysterious parts of the world. Going to these places is not without danger to the messenger, but since the Word is not bound, we cannot be chained by fear of worldly retaliation.

Paul charged the man of God to "preach the word! . . . For the time will come when they will not endure sound doctrine . . . they will turn their ears away from the truth. . . . But you be watchful in all things, endure afflictions, do the work of an evangelist, fulfill your ministry" (2 Timothy 4:2–5). Paul was driven by this message: the love of Christ, His compassion for the souls of men, and the glory of the risen Savior.

The world is a scene of conflict and needs this message. We are under command to proclaim the love of God and the judgment of God, though many will reject it. God has "spoken to us by His Son" (Hebrews 1:2) and said that He will empower His messengers.

As I carried the Gospel throughout the world, I did not expect unqualified success. I was prepared for opposition, resistance, and persecution, and sometimes that occurred. But opposition does not change the fact that God has empowered His Gospel even in the last days. My son Franklin has seen firsthand the evil that reigns in our present world. He has been to some places I had never even heard about until he brought back reports from Christians in hidden areas. His experiences have stirred his passion for getting the Gospel out to all who reject Christ—enemies of the cross. Jesus willingly died for them. How can we not try to reach them with the everlasting Gospel? Paul said, "Woe is me if I do not preach the gospel!" (1 Corinthians 9:16).

Jeremiah was a powerful voice for God's message. This mighty prophet was abused and imprisoned. His life was threatened, and he was always in danger. The persecution began to defeat him in his calling, to the point of agony. He proclaimed,

> I am in derision daily;
> Everyone mocks me.
> Then I said, "I will not make mention of Him,
> Nor speak anymore in His name." (Jeremiah 20:7, 9)

I have never lived under such oppression, nor have most Americans. But Jeremiah felt the heavy weight of God's words and said,

> But His word was in my heart like a burning fire
> Shut up in my bones;
> I was weary of holding it back,
> And I could not.
> But the LORD is with me as a mighty, awesome One.
> Therefore my persecutors will stumble, and will not
>   prevail. (vv. 9, 11)

Jeremiah was weary in body, but it was more wearisome when he tried to suppress the power of God within him. Praise the Lord that he relented and bowed to almighty God, to go forward and preach the Word.

Are we occupying the world with the light of Christ? This is our duty; this is our commission. The King is coming in the twinkling of an eye, one thousandth of a second. This leaves no opportunity for the Christian to recommit his life, the thief to repent, or the prodigal to come home. So we must prepare while there is time—and the time is now!

The editor of a leading American magazine wrote, "A climax of some kind seems to be approaching the world over."[1] This is not a surprise to the people of God. We know what that climax will be, so we should not have a spirit of fear. But the world does live in a state of terror, dread, and alarm for one reason only—their state of disbelief in the One who has predicted all things that will come to pass.

I urge preachers everywhere to take their eyes off of the culture and fix them on the Rock of salvation. Instead of preaching on common unity, preach for our communities to call upon God and repent. If we preach on the common things, let's preach on sin, for it is the one thing that all mankind shares.

When we preach or teach the Scripture, we open the door for the Holy Spirit to do His work. Let's do as Jeremiah did and cast our weariness aside. We have shut up the Word of God when we should have been shouting it out in great victory.

The Gospel is empowered to change lives from the inside out.

The Gospel shows people their wounds and bestows on them love.

It shows them their bondage and supplies the hammer to break open their chains.

It shows them their nakedness and provides them the garments of purity.

It shows them their poverty and pours into their lives the wealth of Heaven.

It shows them their sins and points them to the Savior.

Our chaotic, confused world has no need of more education, more wealth and power, better technology, or unity in diversity. What the world needs before the end comes is the Gospel that will lead them in repentance to the cross of Jesus Christ.

There is coming a day when God's people will be snatched out of the world by the hand of the Lord. The lack of Christ's light will cause a great darkness of evil to fall upon mankind. There will be no comparison to what those days will be like, even with the world's present evil state. But the Preacher from eternity—Jesus Christ, who is the everlasting Gospel—will once again send out His message of love to those who are living in that time.

Then I saw another angel flying in the midst of heaven,
having the everlasting gospel to preach to
those who dwell on the earth—
to every nation, tribe, tongue, and people. (Revelation 14:6)

CHAPTER 31

ETERNAL SALVATION

Reject or Accept

[Jesus] became the author of **eternal** *salvation.*

—HEBREWS 5:9

A YOUNG MAN WAS IN DANGER OF LOSING HIS LIFE TO HEART DISEASE. The doctor told him that his only hope of survival was to have a heart transplant, which would require him to change some bad habits. The patient refused, saying that he didn't have the money. With great compassion, the doctor looked at him and said, "We have the donor organ, and I will pay the cost. Please don't refuse."

The young man grabbed hold of the doctor's arm and said, "Why would you do this when I have brought you so much grief and pain, Dad?"

And the physician-father answered, "Because I love you more than my own life."

To have a spiritual change of heart, you must accept what Jesus

Christ has done and receive this gift offered in love and sacrifice so that you can live. There is no other way to have salvation.

The Great Physician, Jesus Christ, stepped out of Heaven and into our sin-sick world to perform heart surgery on mankind. The book of Hebrews says,

> Today, if you will hear His voice,
> Do not harden your hearts. (3:15)

"Draw near to God and He will draw near to you. Cleanse your hands, you sinners; and purify your hearts" (James 4:8).

God holds in His omnipotent hand the priceless, precious, eternal gift, and He bids you to take it free of charge because His Son—the source of salvation—paid the price with His blood. Salvation is an act of God, initiated by God, wrought by God, and sustained by God.

Many say it is narrow-minded to claim that there is only one way to God. But they make a terrible mistake by suggesting that mere humans can find other ways. It is the Giver of salvation who has proclaimed this unchangeable truth, as Scripture records in John 14:6.

Millions today want salvation, but on their own terms, in their own way. Do we fault surgeons for being narrow-minded when they perform an operation? I doubt it. We depend on their precision, their skill, and their training. No other has done for mankind what Jesus Christ has done because He is the One who saves.

Salvation is what Christ has done for us. It isn't our hold on God that saves us; it is His hold on us. But God will not grant salvation to those who refuse to repent of sin. God does not say be perfect and you will get to Heaven. But He does require that we "continue in the things which you have learned . . . you have known the Holy Scriptures, which are able to make you wise for salvation" (2 Timothy 3:14–15).

Peter wrote of the prophets who inquired and carefully searched the Scriptures concerning the rich promises of salvation in Christ. Imagine the great faith they had in Him who had not yet come to earth, to whom they looked forward with hope. We are blessed to have so much of God's Word fulfilled; it strengthens us as we look forward to what is still ahead:

> An inheritance incorruptible and undefiled . . . reserved in heaven for you.
>
> Though now you do not see Him, yet believing, you rejoice with joy inexpressible and full of glory, receiving the end of your faith—the salvation of your souls. (1 Peter 1:4, 8–9)

We all have a common origin in Adam. It is Adam's blood that courses through every human's veins. There is but one race—the human race—and it suffers from blood poisoning. The blood carries the sentence of death because of Adam's sin. This powerful poison has been passed down from generation to generation since the beginning of time.

A woman wrote to me years ago and scolded me for speaking about the blood of Christ in my sermons. "Jesus never talked about blood," she said. "Why do you have to?" I replied and told her that Jesus not only spoke about blood; He also shed His own for her. "Jesus suffered and died outside the city gates to make his people holy by means of his own blood" (Hebrews 13:12 NLT).

We see the doctrine of the blood throughout the Bible. Peter preached about the blood. Paul wrote about the blood. The redeemed in Heaven will sing about the precious blood. In a sense, the New Testament is the "Book of the Blood" because "without the shedding of blood, there is no forgiveness" (9:22 NLT). It is true that the Bible is bloodstained. "How much more shall the blood of Christ, who through the eternal Spirit offered Himself without [blemish] to God, cleanse your conscience . . . to serve the living God?" (v. 14).

A psychiatrist was interviewed and asked, "Why are there so many suicides?" He answered, "People will do just about anything to get rid of their guilt." I want to proclaim that you don't have to take such drastic measures. Jesus Christ has already died in your place to cover your guilt, shame, and sin of every kind. He already knows what is in your heart. He wants you to confess it, renounce it, and then live for Him.

The Bible says, "Whoever calls on the name of the LORD shall be saved" (Romans 10:13). If you will bring these burdens to Him, He will cleanse you, forgive you, and give you a new heart.

People have poured their hearts out to me with tears because their sins had been discovered. They found themselves in serious trouble, believing there was nowhere to turn for help or comfort. My friend, Jesus is waiting on you, but you have to do the turning. You do have to make a contribution to your salvation—you must receive it. Christ has done the hard part of dying for you, forgiving you, living for you, and praying for you. It is time for a change in your direction; a conscious, deliberate decision to leave sin behind. It means an alteration of attitude, a yielding of the will. The act of repentance does not win any merit or make us worthy to be saved. It only conditions our hearts for receiving the wonderful grace of God.

It is not easy to bend our warped, stubborn wills. But once we do, it will be as though a misplaced vertebra has snapped back into place. Instead of the stress and tension of a life out of harmony with God, the serenity of reconciliation will make you a new person.

Out of a Christian home came a young man who had no interest in Christ. One day his grandfather died unexpectedly. The boy was terribly shaken. He began to search out all the things his parents and grandparents had taught him, and the truth he found led him to salvation in Jesus Christ. People began to see an enormous change in the boy's behavior, even in his countenance. Someone asked him, "Was it your grandfather's death that changed you?"

"No," the boy said, "it was his life."

What a marvelous testimony to a life in Christ well-lived. The grandfather may have never traveled out of his neighborhood, but he lived the Gospel before those in his world.

We have a Father in Heaven who sent His Son to a rebellious and unbelieving world. Jesus Christ brought salvation to us through His Word, through His life, through His death and resurrection, to make it possible for all to obtain this great and eternal gift. His everlasting salvation will never fade or lose its power, for this undying truth will live in the hearts of all those who say yes to Him.

But My salvation will be forever. (Isaiah 51:6)

CHAPTER 32

ETERNAL CROWN

Attending the Great Coronation

JAMES, 1 AND 2 PETER

When he has been approved, he will receive the crown of life which the Lord has promised to those who love Him.

—JAMES 1:12

When the Chief Shepherd appears, you will receive the crown of glory that does not fade away.

—1 PETER 5:4

Work hard to prove that you really are among those God has called. . . . Then God will give you a grand entrance into the **eternal** *Kingdom.*

—2 PETER 1:10–11 NLT

"I AM AN HISTORIAN, I AM NOT A BELIEVER," WROTE H. G. WELLS. "But I must confess . . . that this penniless preacher from Nazareth is irrevocably the very center of history."[1] In his 1920 book *The Outline of History*, he went on to ask, "Is it any wonder that to this day this Galilean is too much for our small hearts?"[2]

Wells, considered one of the most prolific science-fiction writers, believed enough to assert that "this Galilean" captured history; yet he refused to believe He owns it all. Who is the Galilean to which he refers? The same Jesus who walked across the lands of the Bible. This "penniless preacher" has invited the whole world to His coronation. Have you accepted the engraved invitation from the Heavenly palace, sealed with His emblem—the distinguishing mark of His royal blood?

You may say, with a heart like Wells', "I believe in Jesus because history records His existence, but my heart is too small to believe He is the King of all glory." If so, then you have declined the invitation. If you have not let Jesus change your life, then He is not your Lord. The size of your heart matters not; the question is whether He has your whole heart.

To serve the King of kings in the royal palace of Heaven someday, we must first give ourselves wholly to Him on earth and be marked as belonging to Him. "You are a chosen generation, a royal priesthood, a holy nation, His own special people" (1 Peter 2:9). Do you bear this mark?

In the ancient world there were three kinds of people who bore marks on their bodies: soldiers, slaves, and devotees—those who served a person or a cause because they wanted to. Christians have been called to all three. If you have been laughed at because you refused to follow the crowd and compromise the purity that God commands, or if you have been reviled for the name of Christ and brought glory to Him, you bear the marks of Christ. Paul, beaten, imprisoned, and left for dead, said, "I bear in my body the marks of the Lord Jesus" (Galatians 6:17). "Blessed are you," Jesus said, "when they revile and persecute you, and say all kinds of evil against you falsely for My sake. . . . for great is your reward in heaven" (Matthew 5:11–12). We do not live in an ideal world.

The fabric of society is frayed; human nature is laced with rebellion, indifference, and hatred for Christ.

Jesus did not call us to wear a crown in this life. He called us to bear a cross and live for Him in the face of ridicule. When we get to Heaven, though, we will put our crosses down and put on the crowns He gives.

Every earthly ruler has a coronation. But nothing will compare to Christ's coronation in eternity. All who have surrendered to King Jesus will be granted entrance to this great celebration. My place is reserved and paid for by the blood of Christ.

You may ask, "What did you have to do to obtain it?" I had to repent and surrender myself to Him. I did this some eighty years ago, a few days before I turned sixteen. And I have never regretted my decision. One day I will join millions of others to pay allegiance to the King of kings, face-to-face. He has promised that "if we died with Him, / We shall also live with Him. / If we endure, / We shall also reign with Him" (2 Timothy 2:11–12).

While earthly coronations crown one individual, the King of heaven will crown His redeemed congregation: "Be faithful until death, and I will give you the crown of life" (Revelation 2:10). When will this happen? When we stand before the Lord for His evaluation—not for condemnation of sin, for the storm of judgment has passed.

Crossing the North Atlantic years ago, I looked out my porthole and saw the blackest cloud I had ever seen. Certain that we were in for a terrible storm, I asked the steward about it. He said, "Oh, we've already come through it. The storm is behind us."

When we receive salvation, we are forgiven—the storm is behind us. So why, then, does the Bible say believers will appear before the judgment seat of Christ? "We must all appear before the judgment seat of Christ, that each one may receive the things done in the body . . . whether good or bad" (2 Corinthians 5:10). The Lord will judge the living and the dead and will reward the redeemed for how we lived our lives in His name.

He will crown Old Testament saints and martyrs who died for His

Word and His name, and He will crown the church for faithfulness to Him. This is a wonderful eternal promise for believers.

There are actually five crowns mentioned in Scripture. Each crown symbolizes an eternal attribute of Christ.

Those who hold on to eternal life will receive the crown of life. "Blessed is the man who endures temptation; for when he has been approved, he will receive the crown of life which the Lord has promised to those who love Him" (James 1:12).

Soul winners will receive the crown of rejoicing. Paul wrote, "For what is our hope, or joy, or crown of rejoicing? Is it not even you in the presence of our Lord Jesus Christ at His coming? For you are our glory and joy" (1 Thessalonians 2:19–20). Paul rejoiced in seeing others crowned with salvation.

The faithful who live according to God's Word will receive the crown of glory. "Being examples to the flock . . . you will receive the crown of glory that does not fade away" (1 Peter 5:3–4).

Paul also described the "imperishable crown" (1 Corinthians 9:25) in the context of one who competes for an athletic prize. The most coveted wreath of his day was made from the leaves of a wild olive tree. It symbolized virtue and was awarded to the winner in the Olympic Games in Greece. Competitors had to work hard, be disciplined, and play by the rules to contend for the prize.

Olympians understand the rigors of discipline, of bringing their bodies into subjection. Their lives are dominated by physical exercise and mental proficiency. When they compete, they must throw off anything that hinders them.

This is why James tells us to "lay aside all filthiness and overflow of wickedness" (James 1:21) because it weighs us down. No wonder Paul said, "Everyone who competes for the prize is temperate in all things. Now they do it to obtain a perishable crown, but we for an imperishable crown. Therefore. . . . I discipline my body and bring it into subjection" (1 Corinthians 9:25–27).

Living the Christian life is not a game, but it is a competition. There are two teams, only two sides—the enemies of Christ and the soldiers of Christ. And each of us must choose a side.

Moses asked, "Whoever is on the LORD's side—come to me!" (Exodus 32:26). What an invitation! When we are saved out of the world's system, we are instructed to prepare for battle. But the outcome is already decided. The redeemed overcome the enemy, winning an imperishable crown for His honor.

Then there is the crown of righteousness for those who are watching for the Lord's return and working as they wait. Paul said at the end of his life, "Finally, there is laid up for me the crown of righteousness, which the Lord, the righteous Judge, will give to me on that Day, and not to me only but also to all who have loved His appearing" (2 Timothy 4:8).

So while we look forward to receiving these eternal rewards, nothing will give us greater joy than to see Jesus, who made it possible for us to run the race and win. Queen Victoria once heard a sermon on the second coming of Jesus Christ. She was so moved that she told the clergyman later, "I wish He would come during my lifetime so I could lay my crown at His feet."[3] But we will not cast anything perishable at His feet, only that which is incorruptible. This is why we are storing up treasures that have eternal value.

Have you been to a great coronation? Most people have not. When Queen Elizabeth was crowned in 1953, what a dazzling affair it must have been. She walked from the door of Westminster Abbey to the scene of her enthronement, where she was presented with a Bible. The words spoken have been part of the English coronation ceremony since 1689: "Our Gracious Queen; we present You with this *Book*, the most valuable thing that this world affords. Here is Wisdom; This is the Royal Law; These are the lively Oracles of God."[4]

Scripture is the crowning work of the Holy Spirit, and it tells us that when Jesus was born in a stable, He was crowned with rejoicing. Jesus was baptized in the Jordan and was crowned with God's praise. He was tempted in the wilderness but was crowned with power. Jesus was transfigured on the mountain and crowned with glory.

On Palm Sunday Jesus was crowned with blessings as the Messiah. Then on Good Friday he was crowned with thorns. "When they had twisted a crown of thorns, they put it on His head, and a reed in His right hand. And they bowed the knee before Him and mocked Him, saying, 'Hail, King of the Jews!'" (Matthew 27:29).

But no one seemed to know that Sunday was coming. On that glorious Easter morning, Jesus Christ was crowned with resurrected life. "But we see Jesus . . . crowned with glory and honor" (Hebrews 2:9). When He returns, He will be wearing many crowns (Revelation 19:12), and at the end of the age, He will wear the conquering crown. The apostle John wrote of this moment, "Then I looked, and behold, a white cloud, and on the cloud sat One like the Son of Man, having on His head a golden crown, and in His hand a sharp sickle" (14:14).

This, my friends, is the final hour. It is a vital hour. The sickle represents judgment—when Jesus, the Judge, will separate the believers from the unbelievers. The reed that His accusers gave Him to carry up Calvary's hill will become the sovereign scepter he will hold as He judges the human race. The kingdom that Satan built on earth will be doomed, and Christ's kingdom will reign. There will be no more mocking of Jesus Christ, no more mocking of His saints.

We will rejoice to see Him crowned the everlasting King. May our allegiance to Christ be crowned by obedience to His Word.

Now to the King eternal, immortal, invisible, to God who alone is wise, be honor and glory forever and ever. (1 Timothy 1:17)

CHAPTER 33

The Word Eternal

1 John

*We have heard . . . we have seen with our eyes . . .
and our hands have handled . . . the Word of
life . . . and declare to you that **eternal** life.*

—1 John 1:1–2

Dictators fear the Bible, and for good reason: it
inspired Britain's Magna Carta and the United States'
Declaration of Independence. While many nations disbelieve
the Bible, it still remains the most powerful Book ever written because it
is the living Book.

There are those who argue this point, but the universe is sustained
by the Word of God because it is the definitive Word of the Creator.

The Word gave life to everything that was created,
and his life brought light to everyone. (John 1:4 NLT)

God and God's Word are inseparable. A man and his word may be two different things, but eternal God and the eternal Word are the same yesterday, today, and forever. The Bible is a miracle book because it comes from the Miracle Maker.

In many oppressed countries people beg for Bibles; Christians have been persecuted for distributing them. But this Book transcends all generations, all seasons, all cultures, and all races. We don't worship the Bible; we worship the One of whom the Bible speaks because its theme is the unfolding of the great redemptive plan of God through Jesus Christ, His Son, from the beginning of time.

John Wesley, the great evangelist, said, "O give me that book! At any price, give me the book of God. . . . here is knowledge enough for me. Let me be [a man of only one book]."[1] And he was.

Jeremiah wrote of the Book, "Thus speaks the LORD God of Israel, saying: 'Write in a book for yourself all the words that I have spoken to you'" (Jeremiah 30:2).

Most books are born in the minds of authors and documented through the pens of writers. They live a few short years, are put on a shelf, and are often forgotten. But the Holy Bible has been ridiculed, burned, refuted, and trampled on, yet it still goes on forever because it is the living Word of God. "Heaven and earth will pass away, but My words will by no means pass away" (Matthew 24:35). His words matter!

The first words recorded in all of history are in the Bible: "In the beginning" (Genesis 1:1). And God's first words concerning the universe: "Let there be light" (v. 3). His Word is His Light,

> Your word is a lamp to my feet
> And a light to my path. (Psalm 119:105)

Just as God breathed life into Adam, God breathed life into Scripture. His name and His Word are interchangeable. He is the "spoken Word," the "written Word," and the "incarnate Word," as we see in the Gospel of John. "In the beginning was the Word, and the Word was with God, and the Word was God. He was in the beginning with God" (John 1:1–2).

The writer of Hebrews tells the progression of God's Word coming to the human race: God spoke at various times through the prophets; then God spoke to us by His Son, "upholding all things by the word of His power" (1:3).

God has not promised to bless my thoughts, but He has promised to bless His Word. Faith grows when it is planted in the fertile soil of Scripture. I always considered it a lost day if I did not spend time reading at least a passage in this sacred Book. Today I cannot see well enough to read, but I am thankful to have committed much of God's Word to memory. The Bible is a mirror that helps us see our sin. As Christians, we have only one authority and one compass—the Word of God—and it will direct our every thought and step if we rely on Him.

The Word of God is the Work of God. Oh, that we would hunger to be filled with the Word of God, for there is no greater armor, no greater strength, no greater assurance that He is with us and in us. While those around you are filling their minds with bad news, steep yourself in the Good News about God found in His precious Word.

The Word of God convicts us. It cuts, pierces, pricks, smites, severs, carves, and shapes. "For the word of God is living and powerful, and sharper than any two-edged sword, piercing even to the division of soul and spirit, and of joints and marrow, and is a discerner of the thoughts and intents of the heart" (Hebrews 4:12).

The Word of God cleanses. John 15:3 says, "You are already clean because of the word which I have spoken to you." Christ sanctifies and cleanses with the "washing of water by the word" (Ephesians 5:26).

The Word of God gives us new birth. First Peter 1:23 says we have been purified, "having been born again . . . through the word of God which lives and abides forever."

The Word of God keeps us from sin. "Your word I have hidden in my heart, / That I might not sin against You" (Psalm 119:11).

God enables us to live a spiritual life by "every word that proceeds from the mouth of God" (Matthew 4:4).

The Word of God guides our actions. "Blessed are all who hear the word of God and put it into practice" (Luke 11:28 NLT).

The Word of God helps us discern the will of God. God the Spirit will never lead us contrary to the Word of God. I often hear people say, "The Lord led me to do this." I am always a little suspicious unless what the Lord has supposedly said is in keeping with His Word. God will always lead us to do everything that is right because He brought us forth by His own will and His own word (James 1:18).

The Word of God brings rejoicing to our spirits. "God has spoken in His holiness: / 'I will rejoice'" (Psalm 108:7).

The Word of God gives us eternal life. "Have you not read what was spoken to you by God? . . . God is not the God of the dead, but of the living" (Matthew 22:31–32).

The Word of God nourishes our souls. We are told to desire the pure milk of the Word—it enables us to grow (1 Peter 2:2).

> I have treasured the words of His mouth
> More than my necessary food. (Job 23:12)

The Word of God overcomes Satan's power. Jesus quoted Scripture to the devil, and the devil went down. "Away with you, Satan! For it is written, 'You shall worship the LORD your God, and Him only you shall serve'" (Matthew 4:10). We sometimes forget that God is Lord over all, regardless of whether someone chooses to think differently. The Lord's Word is over all things.

The Word of God provides fellowship with Him. The story is told of a young lady who was given a new novel. She struggled to get through it, saying, "It was the driest thing I've ever read." Some months later she met a young man and fell in love. His name had seemed familiar to her, and when she picked up the novel again, she discovered that he had written the book. She began reading it again and couldn't put it down.

What made the difference? She had fallen in love with the author.

The Word of God comforts us in death. "Write: 'Blessed are the dead who die in the Lord.' . . . that they may rest from their labors, and their works follow them" (Revelation 14:13).

The Word of God is the message we preach. The power of the preacher is not in his charisma, his popularity, or even his education; it is in faithfully declaring, "Thus saith the Lord." When I quote Scripture, I know I am quoting the very Word of God. This is why I have always used the phrase, "The Bible says." The Spirit of God takes the Word of God and makes the child of God. Through the written Word we discover the living Word—Jesus Christ.

Paul told Timothy, "Preach the word!" (2 Timothy 4:2). He also said of himself that his preaching was not with words of human wisdom, but words that were packed with Spirit power (1 Corinthians 2:4). Mark wrote of the apostles that they preached everywhere as the Lord confirmed His word (Mark 16:20). Peter proclaimed that "the word of the LORD endures forever," and this is the word that was preached (1 Peter 1:25).

The Word of God brings encouragement. A little boy was silent for a long time, and his mother asked him what he was thinking about. With his head hovering over the pages of the Bible, he answered, "Oh, I'm watching Jesus raise Lazarus from the dead!" How we need to encourage our children to spend time in God's Word. The Bible tells us to "diligently" teach Scripture to our children, to sit and talk with them about it, and then live it in the home (Deuteronomy 6:6–9). This is so important.

The Word of God gives us assurance for Heaven. I can remember as a young man having times of doubt as to my salvation because I compared my experience to others who had emotional conversions. After studying the Bible, however, I gained assurance of my commitment to

Christ, "attaining to all riches of the full assurance of understanding" (Colossians 2:2), because His word is certain.

The Word of God is to be obeyed. "But those who obey God's word truly show how completely they love him. That is how we know we are living in him" (1 John 2:5 NLT).

The Word of God brings blessing. "Blessed is he who reads and those who hear the words of this prophecy, and keep those things which are written in it" (Revelation 1:3).

The Word of God brings hope for the future. "Now I saw heaven opened, and behold, a white horse. And He who sat on him was called Faithful and True. . . . His name is called The Word of God" (19:11–13).

Read God's Word with reverence, for He is holy.

Read it with expectancy, believing God will speak to you.

Read it with dependence on the Holy Spirit, who will open your understanding.

Read it with conviction, to correct and encourage you.

Read it in obedience, so you can put it into action.

Read and then memorize as much as possible, so it will always be with you.

Read it in prayer, so its words will strengthen your faith.

Read and pass it on as a testimony to what God has done for you.

> Your eternal word, O LORD,
> stands firm in heaven. (Psalm 119:89 NLT)

To love the Word is to love God.

To receive the Word is to receive Jesus.

To believe the Word is to believe Christ.

To preach the Word is to proclaim the Gospel of His Word.

You may have heard the expression, "He (or she) is a walking Bible." It is a wonderful thing to hide the Word of God in our hearts; it helps us along the pathway of life. It is important, though, to back it up with our lives. It is a joy to carry in our hands the blessed Scripture and to know where to find various passages. But one day He is coming soon to carry us into His everlasting light, where we will be in the very presence of the Word eternal.

Lord, to whom shall we go? You have the
words of eternal life. (John 6:68)

CHAPTER 34

Everlasting Truth

Tried and Tested

2 AND 3 JOHN

The truth which abides in us . . . will be with us **forever**.
And we also bear witness, and you know that our testimony is true.

—2 JOHN 2, 3 JOHN 12

"THE TRUTH, THE WHOLE TRUTH, AND NOTHING BUT THE TRUTH, SO HELP ME GOD" IS A FAMILIAR OATH. It precedes a sworn testimony given by a witness who has made a commitment to speak truth no matter what. If the witness is later found to have lied while under oath, the person can be charged with the crime of perjury. This is not just in the United States; similar oaths are used in courtrooms in many countries.

In recent years we have seen a great falling away from the truth, and often those who are found to be liars go unpunished. The Bible warns, however, that when judgment comes, so will their punishment; the wrath of God is against such people who "exchanged the truth of God for the lie" (Romans 1:25).

But I want to tell you about "The Truth." He is Jesus Christ, the Son of God and the Savior of the world.

"I tell you the truth" is one of the strongest and frequently used phrases spoken by Jesus.

Jesus knows the lies of the devil. Listen—Satan always uses some of God's truth in his lies. This is his bait. We hear the part that is truth and therefore conclude that the rest is also true—this is trickery of the devil.

Jesus came to destroy the evil lies of Satan, and He patiently waits for His truth to take hold in people's hearts before He returns to strike the last blow on the devil's works.

The great quest for life has always been to find truth. Universities are filled with seekers who want to know the truth. But do they really? Often when they find truth, they reject it because sometimes the truth hurts. So they turn in another direction to find *a* truth that makes them feel better about their defiance of *the* truth.

Jesus did not say we would know *a* truth; He spoke of *the* truth. There may be some truth in various religions and philosophies, but Jesus is *all* truth and *the* Truth. In the same way, the Bible does not contain God's truth; the Bible *is* God's truth. The psalmist declared, "The entirety of Your word is truth" (Psalm 119:160).

If our minds and hearts are not filled with God's truth, something else will take its place: cynicism, occultism, false religions, and philosophies. The list goes on. Where there is truth and error, there is always compromise.

There are those who seek freedom more than the truth. They are free to reject the truth, but the freedom they choose will not set them free. "You shall know the truth, and the truth shall make you free" (John 8:32).

At the end of his life, Buddha said, "I am still searching for truth." This statement could be made by countless scientists, philosophers, and religious leaders throughout history. However, only Jesus Christ made the astonishing claim: "*I am* . . . the truth" (14:6).

Sir Isaac Newton wrote before his death, "I do not know what I may appear to the world, but to myself I seem to have been only like a little boy playing on the seashore, and diverting myself now and then in finding a smoother pebble or a prettier shell than ordinary, whilst the great ocean of truth lay all undiscovered before me."[1]

This "great ocean of truth" is the Word of God. It delivers up the human condition but does not leave us out in the waves to drown—unless we so choose. And many have, and many will. "But know this, that in the last days perilous times will come: For men will be lovers of themselves. . . . always learning and never able to come to the knowledge of the truth" (2 Timothy 3:1–3, 7).

Here is an honest statement: truth is not always pleasant. The reason God judges sin is because He is truth. Like a surgeon, He cuts out all that is false and wrong. His scalpel cuts across all that is dishonest, unfair, and unloving. Isaiah said,

> Woe to those who call evil good, and good evil;
> Who put darkness for light, and light for darkness;
> Who put bitter for sweet, and sweet for bitter.
> (Isaiah 5:20)

For this reason, Jesus plunged into the mire of our sin when He came into this world that He might save us from sin. Then He baptized (drenched) us with the truth of His love that saves, disciplines, and will bring us to Heaven someday. "For this cause I was born, and for this cause I have come into the world, that I should bear witness to the truth" (John 18:37).

All of mankind should be bowing at the mention of His great name, thanking Him for these wonderful truths—someday, all of creation will. "Only fear the LORD, and serve Him in truth with all your heart; for consider what great things He has done for you" (1 Samuel 12:24).

You may say, "What does it matter? What has He done for me? I don't even believe God is real."

Well, it does matter. Whether you believe He is real or not, He is truth. And He has done a great deal for you, whether you acknowledge Him or not. He has given every human being the very breath of life. He has given you the beauty of nature. He has given you talent and intelligence. He has given you opportunity. He has sustained you. And He has offered you His love.

"He makes His sun rise on the evil and on the good, and sends rain on the just and on the unjust" (Matthew 5:45). All of these good things come from Him. This is known as the common grace of God. He also gives you the right to reject Him, though in doing so He retains the right to judge and condemn you to a life forever separated from Him. When that happens, you will know the absolute truth. For the Bible says God's wrath will come to those "who suppress the truth in unrighteousness" (Romans 1:18). And those who spend eternity in Hell will have no doubt why they are there—"they did not receive the love of the truth, that they might be saved. . . . They all may be condemned who did not believe the truth but had pleasure in unrighteousness" (2 Thessalonians 2:10–12).

God's courtroom will be arrayed in the light of the truth, just as it was when Jesus was brought to trial and given the opportunity to defend Himself. Pilate asked, "What is truth?" (John 18:37) after Jesus had told him, "Everyone who is of the truth hears My voice" (v. 38).

Now, the opposite of truth is falsehood. Exodus 20:16 tells us that we should not lie ("bear false witness"). There is a great gulf between the Truth and the lie—Jesus Christ, the Truth, and Satan, the father and author of lies. "[The devil] was a murderer from the beginning, and does not stand in truth, because there is no truth in him. When he speaks a lie, he speaks from his own resources, for he is a liar and the father of it" (John 8:44).

Satan assaults with his lies, and believing them will lead to his eternal fire. He has already appeared in the courtroom of truth and received his sentence: he will be "cast into the lake of fire and brimstone. . . . [and] will be tormented day and night forever and ever" (Revelation 20:10). This is his indictment. His days are numbered. He is on death row awaiting his ultimate fate. Mankind is navigating through life with unreliable direction. Satan is telling you to go his way. Refuse to listen!

People today have found comfort in relying on GPS to get where they are going safely and on time. But there are studies that indicate it is not difficult to generate false position reports. The question is asked, "If a GPS receiver reports its position to a monitoring center using a radio signal, how do we know that the receiver is telling the truth?" We can't—until we arrive at the destination.

Truth is important in navigation. A pilot trains for hours to keep from making one fatal error—just one. And his or her training never stops.

Truth is important in mathematics too. There can be no guesswork or speculation in architectural equations.

Truth is important in chemistry. If you use the wrong formula, you will not get a true reaction.

I have met people who are habitual liars. They have lied so long they can no longer distinguish between truth and a lie. Scripture says of such people, "They will turn their ears away from the truth, and be turned aside to fables" (2 Timothy 4:4). Their sensitivity to sin has been almost, if not completely, deadened. But the Gospel truth tells us to show Christ's love and correct "those who are in opposition . . . [so] God perhaps will grant them repentance, so that they may know the truth" (2:25).

Truth matters. And just because truth is unpopular doesn't mean that it should not be proclaimed.

It is Satan's purpose to steal the seed of truth from your heart by sending distracting and deceptive thoughts. The difference between a Christian and a non-Christian is that though both may have good and evil thoughts, Christ gives His followers discernment and the power to choose the right rather than the wrong. The Holy Spirit takes God's word of truth and ministers to our deepest needs. And the person who discovers truth has a serenity, peace, and certainty that others do not have. "Every good gift and every perfect gift is from above. . . . He brought us forth by the word of truth" (James 1:17–18).

Truth is timeless. It does not differ from one age to another, from one people to another, from one geographical location to another. The great all-prevailing Truth stands for time and eternity. And we will see Him in all His glory when He charges from eternity past into eternity present. His name is Faithful and True (Revelation 19:11), and He will reign from the City of Truth (Zechariah 8:3).

And the truth of the LORD endures forever. (Psalm 117:2)

CHAPTER 35

THE ETERNAL FLAME

Snatching Souls from the Fire

JUDE

Those cities were destroyed by fire and serve as a
*warning of the **eternal** fire of God's judgment.*

—JUDE 7 NLT

"ETERNAL FLAMES HAVE BURNED FOR CENTURIES." That's what the headline read. In fact, such sites attract tourists and curiosity seekers from around the world.

The Eternal Fire of Baba Gurgur, located at the center of the enormous oil field in Iraq, is said to have burned for thousands of years. The flames are created by natural gas that percolates up through the rocks. In the Himalayas another eternal flame burns at Jwalamukhi Temple in India. Its blue flames are fueled by burning natural gas that comes from the rock sanctum of the temple, where the flame itself is worshiped as deity. Then there's Burning Mountain. Scientists believe this to be the oldest known continuous underground fire. Located in New South

Wales, Australia, this coal-burning fire is believed to have been going strong for six thousand years.[1]

A fire ignited in 1688 at Brennender Berg in Saarland, Germany, still burns today. Poet Johann Wolfgang von Goethe visited there in 1770 and wrote that the dense steam escaped through the crevices and he could feel the hot ground even through the thick soles of his shoes.[2]

The legendary fire of Mrapen is located in Indonesia. It is reported that the flame never extinguishes, not even in the middle of rain or winds. First recorded in the fifteenth century, this natural gas leak comes from deep underground and burns to this day. There are others, of course. Olympos Mountain, near Antalya, Turkey, is home to a flame that does not die by day or by night.[3]

One of the most daunting sites is found in the middle of the Karakum Desert of Turkmenistan and is known as the "Door to Hell." Its fire has burned since the 1970s.[4] These are not fantasies from the latest Hollywood movie. They are real places and real fires that don't die out and cannot be put out.

In all of these cases scientists cannot say how the fires started; they just cropped up. After preaching a message on this subject some years ago, I received a letter from someone in the Canadian Rockies. He said that even after a forest fire is put out, it is not unusual for remnants of the fire to smolder for weeks, even months, underground. "There is no human way for underground fires to be extinguished," he said, "even if firefighters knew the exact locations."

Fire is mysterious and fascinating. It can purify or destroy. It can glow or rage. It can dance on a wick or snuff out a life.

Fire can also be useful. There is nothing more inviting than a crackling fire on a cold winter's night. Shepherds and cowboys have huddled around campfires throughout history. Branding fires marked ownership of livestock. Jesus prepared breakfast over a fire on the shore of Galilee for His disciples (John 21:1–13). Then there is the refiner's fire used to purify gold. When all the impurities are gone, the result is 24-karat gold—the most valuable grade.

The Lord used the effect of fire to encourage the believer in Christ. "There is wonderful joy ahead, even though you must endure many trials for a little while. These trials will show that your faith is genuine. It is being tested as fire tests and purifies gold—though your faith is far more precious than mere gold" (1 Peter 1:6–7 NLT).

Fire also brings hazard to life and property. The lick of flames speaks terror, anguish, destruction, and loss. I remember one day when my son was a boy. As I was passing through the kitchen, I found him lighting matches and said, "Franklin, if I ever catch you playing with fire again, I'll spank you."

The next day he was right back in the kitchen lighting matches. I said, "Didn't I tell you that if you played with matches again you would get a spanking?"

His eyes twinkled as he said, "No, Daddy. You said, if you ever *catch* me." And he ran outside and up into the hills, escaping punishment for a time.

The Bible speaks frequently of fire—more than five hundred times—and warns unrepentant sinners of Hellfire. The first fire destroyed the cities of Sodom and Gomorrah. The full account is in the book of Genesis, but in one of the very last books of the New Testament, we read the letter written by Jude, the half brother of Jesus. "And don't forget Sodom and Gomorrah . . . which were filled with immorality and every kind of sexual perversion. Those cities were destroyed by fire and serve as a warning of the eternal fire of God's judgment" (v. 7 NLT).

Why did Jude go all the way back to the beginning of time when he was writing to New Testament believers? He says to us,

> I . . . [urge] you to defend the faith that God has entrusted once for all time to his holy people. I say this because some ungodly people have wormed their way into your churches, saying that God's marvelous grace allows us to live immoral lives. The condemnation of such people was recorded long ago. (vv. 3–4 NLT)

This brief book has firepower that set off a twenty-five-verse alarm. Jude's purpose was to warn of deceivers who portray themselves as followers of Christ but do not obey His commands. This is a book of caution. God gives people fair warning.

Now there are those who believe that the fire of Hell is symbolic; others claim Hellfire can burn without consuming. We read the remarkable story of the burning bush that was not consumed, and Moses heard the voice of God in the fire. We see the miraculous story of the three Hebrews who were thrown into the fiery furnace and came out unharmed because the Lord was in the fire with them.

I can say with certainty that if there is no literal fire in Hell, then God is using symbolic language to indicate something far worse. Just as there are no words to adequately describe the grand beauty of Heaven, we cannot begin to imagine just how horrible the place called Hell is.

Jude wrote:

Ungodly men . . . turn the grace of our God into lewdness and deny . . . our Lord Jesus Christ.

They corrupt themselves. Woe to them! . . .

They are . . . wandering stars for whom is reserved the blackness of darkness forever. . . .

"Behold, the Lord comes . . . to execute judgment on all, to convict all who are ungodly . . . of all their ungodly deeds which they have committed in an ungodly way, and of all the harsh things which ungodly sinners have spoken against Him."

Mockers . . . walk according to their own ungodly lusts. (vv. 4, 10–13, 14–15, 18)

Jude's use of repetition is fierce. His heart burned red hot. Like a marksman with a round of ammunition, he is relentless in targeting the ungodly acts of sinners. In two sentences he uses the word *ungodly* five times. But lest you think Jude is uncaring, listen to his plea.

But you, dear friends, must build each other up in your most holy faith, pray in the power of the Holy Spirit, and await the mercy of our Lord Jesus Christ, who will bring you eternal life. In this way, you will keep yourselves safe in God's love.

And you must show mercy to those whose faith is wavering. Rescue others by snatching them from the flames of judgment. Show mercy to still others, but do so with great caution, hating the sins that contaminate their lives. (vv. 20–23 NLT)

Jude emphasizes the ungodly acts and then applies the Gospel salve—mercy. Mercy is mentioned three times in two short sentences.

So what is he asking believers to do? Jude warns them to defend the faith and beware of deceivers who try to change truth for a lie. He boldly proclaims that they "do not have God's Spirit in them" (v. 19 NLT).

He tells them to remember times past when God warned that continuing in sin would bring judgment, yet He patiently waited, giving people the chance to turn away from evil. Jude reviews the behavior that incites the eternal fire of judgment and the behavior that awards eternal life.

Then he speaks about those who have been misled by deceivers, telling them to show mercy because even the deceivers' hearts may still be reached with the Gospel truth. He urgently implores others to pull sinners from the fire who are almost committed to believing the lie. But he warns them to beware, for in doing so they themselves can be contaminated (influenced) by sin, and also fall into the fire (v. 23).

Sin is a burning fire. It inflames temptation, sears the conscience, sets the heart ablaze with lust, and scorches the soul.

Sin is also like a fire in that it can be both visibly active and concealed within. We see this with King David when he looked at Bathsheba. His lust smoldered and then ignited a firestorm of adultery, lies, deception, and premeditated murder. The Bible warns that when we cave to temptation, we are drawn away from God. The evil we do brings death (James 1:14–15).

Sin always lies. God hates the lying tongue that corrupts (Proverbs 6:17). James wrote, "See how great a forest a little fire kindles! And the tongue is a fire, a world of iniquity. The tongue is so set among our members that it defiles the whole body, and sets on fire the course of nature; and it is set on fire by hell" (3:5–6).

I remember years ago appearing on the *Phil Donahue Show* before a live audience. Phil asked me, "Why do we have to put sin in the heart of a little baby?" I answered, "Phil, I didn't say that. God said it. The Bible says that we are all born with the sin nature" (Psalm 51:5). Donahue seemed stunned, then asked the audience if they agreed. Most did.

Sin in its active state, like fire, can illuminate and attract. Moths are attracted to candle flames. Flies are lured by lightbulbs. People are attracted to the mystery of sin before they are aware that the flame has pulled them to the scene of the crime. Men and women are attracted to the flicker of lust and, in time, are pulled in by the raging blaze. Temptation smolders and then ignites. Sin is like fire because of the way it destroys.

The Bible continually warns of the coming judgment. But God, in mercy, sent His Son to rescue us from the flames of Hell. "For this purpose the Son of God was manifested, that He might destroy the works of the devil" (1 John 3:8). And God keeps His promises. The devil and his demons will be committed to the fires of Hell.

Jude has turned the siren on full blast. He has sounded the alarm for slumbering believers and sent them on a rescue mission—to pull souls from the everlasting flames. God does not want anyone to go to this awful place.

I know there are people who say, "A loving God would not send people to Hell." But my friend, it is because of His love that He gives us advance warning. He extends His mercy beyond human comprehension. The world is on fire, and we are God's firemen. We have been given the tool for the rescue mission—the water of life that flows from the Savior. It is able to quench the fiery darts of the wicked and drench the sin that otherwise would destroy. God would rather transform the sinner than send him into everlasting punishment. Everyone has this personal choice to make, because Jesus Christ is a personal Savior.

Believers, take to heart what Jude has written. Take hold of someone who is a step away from the fire of the everlasting flame. People may resent you for caring about their eternal state, but warn them anyway. Often they don't want to be warned because it necessitates making a decision. People enjoy doing the unnecessary and hate doing the necessary. Avoiding the eternal fire is imperative.

When Jesus was in Capernaum preaching in the synagogue, a man possessed by a demon shouted at Jesus to go away and leave him alone. The man said, "Did You come to destroy us? I know who You are— the Holy One of God!" (Luke 4:34). But Jesus did not leave him alone. He rebuked the demon and ordered him out of the man. The man was snatched from the fire.

So when some say, "It's none of your business," a friend will answer:

- If you're drowning, I will not leave you alone. I have the Gospel lifeboat.
- If you are starving, I will not leave you alone. I have the Bread of life.
- If you have ingested poison, I will not leave you alone. I have the Gospel antidote.
- If you are lost in darkness, I will not leave you alone. I have the Light of the Gospel.
- If you are sick, I will not leave you alone. I will point you to the Great Physician.
- If you are on the wrong road, I will not leave you alone. I will show you the Way.
- If you are on a wild sea, I will not leave you alone. I will point you to the Lighthouse.
- If you are in bondage, I will not leave you alone. I have the liberty to tell you that Truth can set you free.

James wrote, "He who turns a sinner from the error of his way will save a soul from death" (5:20). We must use every opportunity to send out the powerful warning that burned within Jude. Then he ended his letter with a description of eternity that glows not from fire but from the light of God Himself.

All glory to him who alone is God, our Savior
through Jesus Christ our Lord.
All glory, majesty, power, and authority are
his before all time, and in the present,
and beyond all time! Amen. (Jude 25 NLT)

CHAPTER 36

THE KING'S ETERNAL REIGN

The Cradle, the Cross, and the Crown

REVELATION

The kingdoms of this world have become the kingdoms of . . . Christ, and He shall reign **forever and ever!**

—REVELATION 11:15

NO WONDER HE WAS A CARPENTER.

Cradled in a manger made of wood, He brought Christmas joy to the world at His birth.

He is Jesus.

Nailed to an old rugged cross and lifted up to die for sin, He brought Easter glory to the world by His resurrection.

He is the Savior.

Coming again as the Branch of righteousness, He will bring an ever-lasting kingdom and will reign in power.

Behold! His name is the Branch.

Why Branch? At the time of Jesus' birth, the royal line of David—from which He came—had dried up in Israel. But He would still be King, for Branch is a title for Messiah and speaks of fruitfulness. The prophet Isaiah said,

> There shall come forth a Rod from the stem of Jesse,
> And a Branch shall grow out of his roots. (Isaiah 11:1)

When Jesus stepped down from His eternal throne, He came as Servant—the Vine of the Vinedresser—who brings life. The Child from Heaven had royal blood in His veins, though He was born in a stable. But when He comes back, "the Lord God will give Him the throne of His father David. And He will reign . . . forever, and of His kingdom there will be no end" (Luke 1:32–33).

This is why the prophet Zechariah prophesied that the Messiah would come from David's royal lineage and said, "Behold, the Man whose name is the BRANCH!" (Zechariah 6:12). No wonder the Branch will then say, "*I am* . . . your King" (Isaiah 43:15).

It is hard to grasp that a King would serve, but this is no ordinary king. This is Jesus, whose Father proclaimed, "I am bringing forth My Servant the Branch."

He will be gloriously crowned. He will sit on His righteous throne and "from His place He shall branch out" (Zechariah 6:12)—to serve.

How will He serve? He will harvest His bounty—souls to fill Heaven.

No wonder the Bible has a lot to say about roots, seeds, branches, and vines—and trees. I can't help but wonder what went through the mind of Jesus as He worked in the carpenter's shop, filled with varied woods harvested from the forests. We certainly know that He spoke of trees

THE KING'S ETERNAL REIGN

to illustrate truth as He walked the valleys and hills with His disciples. Nearly every biblical writer wrote about the trees. Perhaps this is why Ezekiel described the coming kingdom this way:

> Trees of all kinds will grow along both sides of the river. The leaves of these trees will never turn brown and fall, and there will always be fruit on their branches. . . . They [will be] watered by the river flowing from the Temple. The fruit will be for food and the leaves for healing. (47:12 NLT)

This is certainly a picture of the coming King: from the root of Jesse, from the seed of David, whose name is Branch. No wonder Jesus called Himself the true Vine—"*I am* the vine; you are the branches" (John 15:5)—for eternal life flows from the vine to the branches. This is Heaven's family tree.

No wonder Jesus found strength as He kneeled among the olive trees in the garden of Gethsemane, at the base of the Mount of Olives. On this mountain, overlooking Jerusalem, Jesus taught His disciples to pray. This is where He wept over the city. This is where He will plant His feet when He comes back in glory.

Then His kingdom will branch out—just as the crown of a tree, by its branches, covers a great area. The Branch protects and hovers over His own, and "His beauty shall be like an olive tree" (Hosea 14:6).

Years ago I preached a sermon titled "The Cradle, the Cross, and the Crown." But there is no greater sermon than what is found in Isaiah when He prophesied the tremendous life of the Lord Jesus Christ.

The Babe would be named Immanuel, God with us (Isaiah 7:14). Jesus was born among His very creation, and it isn't hard to imagine the animals bowing in reverence as they welcomed the Child who would be King into the world.

Isaiah wrote:

> For He shall grow up . . . as a tender plant,
> And as a root out of dry ground. . . .
> He was wounded for our transgressions. (53:2–5)

And He died with a crown of thorns piercing His brow. But Job wrote:

> There is hope for a tree,
> If it is cut down, that it will sprout again,
> And that its tender shoots will not cease. (14:7)

The world thought they had conquered the King of the Jews when they crucified Him, but Peter wrote that while Jesus bore our sins in His own body "on the tree" (1 Peter 2:24), the seed would live again—and He did. No wonder the Branch is coming back to reign (Isaiah 9:7).

This is eternity—it is coming. Revelation is a book that thrills the heart. It is a book of action because its message calls out to mankind with repetition: Behold! And come!

Why? There is something magnificent to behold that is yet to come!

The apostle John is told, "[Come up here—come and see!] Behold, the Lion of the tribe of Judah, the Root of David" (Revelation 5:5). Then we're told that Heaven will come down and to hold fast till the Lord comes. The nations will gather and come to worship Him. No wonder the Spirit tells us to come; let him who thirsts come drink, and the Lord proclaims, "Behold, I make all things new" (21:5).

Behold! "The marriage of the Lamb has come" (19:7).

Come! "Gather together for the supper of the great God" (v. 17).

Where does the King want us to come? Home.

This little word *come* is filled with eternal promise. I suppose that is why I have always been drawn to the song that closed most of our evangelistic crusades:

And as thou bidst me come to Thee,
O Lamb of God, I come, I come.[1]

Jesus gives us His words:

"*I am* the Alpha and the Omega, the Beginning and the End . . .
who is and who was and who is to come." (Revelation 1:8)

"I, Jesus, have sent My angel to testify to you these things. . . .
I am the Root and the Offspring of David, the Bright and
Morning Star." (22:16)

He who testifies to these things says, "Surely I am coming
quickly." (v. 20)

He sends out a mighty promise: "He who overcomes . . . I will write
on him My new name" (3:12).

The Bible says, "He is Lord of lords and King of kings; and those
who are with Him are called, chosen, and faithful" (17:14). The chosen
are those who have received Him as personal Savior. When we are with
Him for eternity, we will inherit a new address—Heaven—and it is all
the address we'll need. We will also inherit our new names. And we will
eat the fruit from the Vine of the tree that possesses eternal life in Christ
Jesus our Lord.

No wonder He came—that we might come.

The great revelation for me is to know that when the Lord calls me
home, *where I am* then, is where He will be, waiting in the place He has
prepared from the beginning. This is the Eternal Reign of the Great I Am.

No wonder He is King!

I am He who lives . . . and behold, I am
alive forevermore. (Revelation 1:18)

NOTES

Foreword

1. CBS News, "How We See Heaven and Hell," *Sunday Morning*, October 26, 2014, www.cbsnews.com/news/how-we-see-heaven-and-hell/2/.
2. Billy Graham, *The Reason for My Hope: Salvation* (Nashville: W Publishing, 2013).

Introduction

1. Dana Blanton, "10/28/05 Fox News Poll: More Believe in Heaven than Hell," FoxNews.com, October 28, 2005, http://www.foxnews.com/story /2005/10/28/102805-fox-poll-more-believe-in-heaven-than-hell.html.
2. Blood, Sweat & Tears, vocal performance of "And When I Die," by Laura Nyro, Columbia 4-45008, 1969, 45 rpm.

Chapter 1: Tree of Eternal Life

1. Joseph Addison, *Cato: A Tragedy in Five Acts* (1823; repr. Project Gutenburg e-book, 2010), Act V, scene 1, http://www.gutenberg.org/files /31592/31592-h/31592-h.htm.
2. Hannah Arendt, "The Concept of History: Ancient and Modern," *The Portable Hannah Arendt*, ed. Peter Baehr (New York: Penguin, 2000), 278.
3. William Shakespeare, *Antony and Cleopatra* (1606; repr. OpenSource Shakespeare [George Mason University]), Act V, scene 2, lines 3739–40, http://www.opensourceshakespeare.org/views/plays/play_view. php?WorkID=antonycleo&Act=5&Scene=2&Scope=scene.

4. Walter A. Maier, "The Resurrection Reality," sermon preached Easter Day 1937, http://media.lhm.org/lutheranhour/mp3s/historic_resurrectionreality_1937_wam.mp3.

Chapter 3: One Eternal Sacrifice

1. Charlotte Elliott, "Just As I Am" (music by William B. Bradbury), 1835; Cyberhymnal.org, http://cyberhymnal.org/htm/j/u/justasam.htm.

Chapter 5: Power Forever

1. "Pocket Testament League in Formosa," *Moody Church News* 36:8 (1951).

Chapter 7: Eternal King, Eternal Throne, Eternal Kingdom

1. Quoted in an August 21, 1998, letter by William W. Quinn, Lt. Gen., US Army (Ret.); www.arlingtoncemetery.net/wwquinn.htm.

Chapter 10: Joy Eternal

1. Virgil P. Brock and Blanche K. Brock, "Beyond the Sunset," © 1936 by The Rodeheaver Co. © Renewed 1964 by The Rodeheaver Co., owner; quoted on Hymnal Accompanist website, www.hymnalaccompanist.com/oldhymns/CH865.html.

Chapter 12: Eternity Set in the Heart

1. The full text of my remarks can be found in the archives of the Richard Nixon Library, "Funeral Services of Mrs. Nixon," Richard Nixon Library and Birthplace Foundation, https://archive.is/JfDpy.
2. Burt Meyers, "The Silent Partner," *Time*, February 29, 1960, 25.
3. Tricia Nixon Cox's remark was made in a long-ago interview with *The Guardian*. Julie Nixon Eisenhower's statement was contained in her biography, *Pat Nixon: The Untold Story* (New York: Simon & Schuster, 1986; now available in a Kindle edition from Renaissance Literary & Talent).

Chapter 14: Everlasting Love

1. Blaise Pascal, quoted in Joshua Mendes, "Booze for Bolsheviks, A Billion Hours of Driving, the Odds on God, and Other Matters. It's Not Fair," *Fortune*, January 7, 1985, http://archive.fortune.com/magazines/fortune/fortune_archive/1985/01/07/65458/index.htm.

2. Sigmund Freud, *Civilization and Its Discontents*, tr. and ed. James Strachey, Standard Edition (New York: W. W. Norton & Company, 1930), XXI.101.

3. Victor Hugo, *Les Misérables*, tr. Isabel F. Hapgood, chapter 4, on The Literature Network, www.online-literature.com/victor_hugo /les_miserables/43/.

Chapter 15: Everlasting Peace

1. Manie P. Ferguson, "Blessed Quietness" (music by W. S. Marshall), c. 1897; http://library.timelesstruths.org/search/?query=music&q =jesus+speaks+peace+to+me.

Chapter 18: Eternal Prayer Answered

1. Donald Grey Barnhouse, in Charlie "Tremendous" Jones and Bob Kelly, *The Tremendous Power of Prayer* (West Monroe, LA: Howard, 2000), 66.

Chapter 19: Eternal Rewards

1. Norman P. Grubb, *C. T. Studd: Cricketeer and Pioneer* (1933; repr. Fort Washington, PA: Christian Literature Crusade, 1982), 118.

2. Howard Culbertson, "No Reserves. No Retreats. No Regrets," Christian Missions (Southern Nazarene University), http://home.snu.edu/~hculbert /regret.htm.

Chapter 25: The Cross Everlasting

1. Quoted in Michael Battle, *Practicing Reconciliation in a Violent World* (New York: Morehouse, 2005), 2.

Chapter 26: The Church Eternal

1. HELPS Word-studies, s.v. Strong's NT 1577 (*ekklésia*); Bible Hub, http:// biblehub.com/greek/1577.htm.

Chapter 30: The Everlasting Gospel

1. David Lawrence, *U. S. News and World Report*, quoted in John Wesley White, "Rapture Ready," www.raptureready.com/terry/james32.html.

Chapter 32: Eternal Crown

1. This is an often-quoted saying that has been widely attributed to H. G. Wells. It was possibly written late in his life.
2. H. G. Wells, *The Outline of History: Being a Plain History of Life and Mankind* Kindle edition (1920; repr. Amazon Digital Services, 2014), Kindle ed., book 4, ch. 30, 581.
3. G. P. Eckman, "Queen Victoria's Heart," in *One Thousand Evangelistic Illustrations*, sp. ed., Aquilla Webb (New York: George H. Doran, 1921), 278.
4. *The Coronation Service According to the Use of the Church of England*, ed. John Fuller Russell (London: Basil Mantagu Pickering, 1857), 19.

Chapter 33: The Word Eternal

1. John Wesley, *Sermons on Several Occasions*, preface, in *John Wesley*, Albert C. Outler, ed. (New York: Oxford University Press, 1980), 89.

Chapter 34: Everlasting Truth

1. Sir Isaac Newton, quoted in G. W. Curtis, "Education and Local Patriotism," *Readings on American State Government*, Paul Samuel Reinsh, ed. (Boston: Ginn and Company, 1911), 330.

Chapter 35: The Eternal Flame

1. Patrick Weidinger, "10 Natural Eternal Flames You've Never Heard Of," ListVerse, http://listverse.com/2013/08/15/10-natural-eternal-flames -youve-never-heard-of/.
2. Ibid.
3. Ibid.
4. "9 Naturally Occurring Eternal Flames," PhotoBlog, September 12, 2014, www.mnn.com/earth-matters/wilderness-resources/blogs /9-naturally-occurring-eternal-flames.

Chapter 36: The King's Eternal Reign

1. Charlotte Elliott, "Just As I Am Without One Plea," Cyberhymnal.org, http://cyberhymnal.org/htm/j/u/justasam.htm.

ABOUT THE AUTHOR

Billy Graham, world-renowned preacher, evangelist, and author, has delivered the Gospel message to more people face-to-face than anyone in history and has ministered on every continent of the world, in more than 185 countries. Millions have read his inspirational classics, including *Angels, Peace with God, The Holy Spirit, Hope for the Troubled Heart, How to Be Born Again, The Journey, Nearing Home*, and *The Reason for My Hope: Salvation*.